More Than a Mile

What America Needs from Local Food

Nicholas R. Carter

ISBN: 978-17-91728-92-2

"Agriculture ... is our wisest pursuit, because it will in the end contribute most to real wealth, good morals & happiness."

—Thomas Jefferson, 1787

Table of Contents

Author's Note

I've heard it said: A fish is the last one to know that it's wet. In my own case, I was the last one to know that I am a farmer at heart. I shouldn't have been, of course. For the first 18 years of my life, I was a farmer. It was wrapped up in my identity. As a teenager, my social life revolved around feeding schedules for my dairy herd. My first car was a truck. And, I won more trophies with 4-H livestock than I did playing school sports.

Farming was such an embedded part of my life that I didn't realize how significant a change it would be for me to leave.

At age 18, I headed off to college without a second thought. Like most American teens, I picked a school of study that would lead to a good career, packed my bags, and off I went. The seemingly obvious career—to be a farmer—was not an option on the table. There was hardly an income left for my dad on our small, family farm, much less one for me to find by joining the enterprise.

Nearly a decade later, after having built a successful software business, a family, and a life in Indianapolis, I was restless.

Not just restless in the way that adventurers and thrill-seekers are restless, seeking something bigger and better. No, instead I was restless for something smaller and simpler.

I was ready to leave the office, the book signings, and the podiums behind. I wanted to get my hands dirty again. Literally.

I didn't want to go back, per se. I didn't want to return to a nostalgic memory of home. I was happy in Indianapolis. Even as I write this, I still am quite happily planted in Indianapolis with no plans to return to live on the farm where I was raised. But I did want to revisit that pivotal decision that an 18-year old fish made before he knew he was wet. I wanted to examine its impact, not for going backward, but for what it meant going forward.

I couldn't imagine starting a new farm, either. In my late twenties, successful though I was, I couldn't muster the capital to buy a few thousand acres of land, a combine, and a tractor. There are no first-generation farmers in America today—at least, not of the style of farming that farms like Dad's had tried to become.

I was an entrepreneur, however, which meant I had trained myself to be keen to market opportunities. It was 2011 and the local food trend had caught my attention. While the quaint, small nature of local farmers markets and niche food shops seemed foreign to the grain farming I had experienced, the local food movement had one redeeming quality: It was open to me.

There was one small problem, however. It's called "local food," not farming, and I knew only about farming. I was completely ignorant of all things regarding food. I was hardly a local food consumer, much less a purveyor. I didn't know the regulations, the market forces, the customers nor the suppliers. I had never even attended a farmers market, didn't know what the acronym CSA stood for, and had never heard of names of famous American farmers like Joel Salatin or Wendell Berry.

Over the course of the last seven years, I changed the trajectory of my career. I re-imagined that decision to leave the farm and moved forward with intentional course corrections.

In the local food industry, my grain farming experience didn't apply. Marketing and sales were the only skill I thought I had to offer. So, I built local food distributor. As that grew, I partnered with two other local food entrepreneurs to create a local food processor. We put local food on the shelves of over 300 grocery stores around the Midwest. It wasn't until that company was acquired in 2016 that I saw the opportunity to bring my technology skills to bear on local food.

Outside the farming world, I was a software guy—starting and building tech-startups in a digital world where the internet is everything. As it turns out, those two worlds were colliding in ways I hadn't realized before.

I built an online farmers market—using technology to connect consumers directly with local producers. The mission was simple: to enable food producers to thrive in their local and regional markets. We would leverage technology to bring local farmers the kinds of automation, logistics, and marketplace access that had once been reserved only for the largest, most industrious supermarkets and food giants.

As the market grew, something unexpected happened. Dad signed up as a vendor. Yes, dad—the grain farmer turned factory worker. On the very land where I had learned to farm industrial-scale grain and confined animals, dad started producing local food.

The business, in a way, led me home.

While I know I cannot return to our family farm and redo the path my own career has taken, I do know this: When my own son is 18, I want that choice to be his. The choice to farm should never be, for anyone in America, a foregone negative conclusion.

4

You Gonna Eat That?

I was standing behind a small table in the frozen food aisle at Whole Foods Market, asking every passer-by, "Have you tried our Indiana Sweet Corn?"

That summer, I had started freezing locally-grown vegetables and distributing them in grocery stores. I was on a mission to increase access to local food. I believed, at the time, that getting more local food on the grocery store shelves was the answer. So, there I was, in a grocery aisle, my product on the shelf next to me. It was a dream come true.

"Is it organic?" one customer asked me before she accepted a sample. She was a short woman, probably in her fifties, with greying hair and thick glasses.

"Our suppliers are small, local farmers. They are not certified organic, but they use organic practices," I answered with a smile.

She didn't look convinced. She looked over my whole display, top to bottom, with the kind of scrutiny that you might expect while buying knock-off sunglasses from a street vendor. Then she noticed that the bag was stamped "Non-GMO" right on the front. "So, you're Non-GMO verified?"

"Yes, we have been certified for that." We had undergone an audit to get a third-party validation of our claim that the corn was not a genetically modified organism (GMO).

"So," she followed up, "it's not sprayed with anything?"

After a brief pause, during which my mouth stood agape while I chose my next words, I finally blurted out, "That's not what non-GMO means."

"You said organic, or organic *practices*. That means it's never been sprayed."

Now, before I move on it's important for me to point out in case you are unaware, that her claim is entirely untrue. Organic, at least the definition of organic from the USDA Certified Organic program, absolutely does not preclude spraying pesticides, herbicides, and spreading fertilizers. What it *does* mean is that those materials must all be "organic" pesticides, herbicides, and fertilizers. That is, they must be chemicals that are found and produced in nature, and not synthetic. (And, even that requirement has been loosened over time, but more on that in a later chapter.)

For now, just know one thing that I value very highly—perhaps too highly—in life: I was right, and she was wrong. So, despite conventional wisdom regarding customer service, I persisted.

"No. That isn't what organic means." I contested. I went on with an ill-timed lecture, "A Non-GMO corn plant has no defense against insects. In Indiana, in our climate, if it's not sprayed with BT every 2 to 3 days it will be pure worms."

"What's BT?" She asked skeptically.

"I can't remember what it stands for," I started. (Incidentally, it's Bacillus Thuringiensis. But that's not important now.) I continued, "But it's a kind of bacteria that's lethal to the moths…"

"BACTERIA?" She interrupted me.

This was not going well.

"Yes, that's an 'organic' method of keeping pests away." I put air quotes around "organic." Now my tone was starting to sound a bit too snarky.

At that point it was abundantly clear that she was not going to become a customer. Good salespeople know that you cannot "tell" to "sell." I was not a good salesperson that day. I couldn't resist continuing my pitch.

I took the bag and turned it over to the back. Pointing to a small blurb at the bottom of the bag, I said, "this is the farmer that grew this corn. His name is Jeremy. If you follow this website here, you can ask Jeremy any questions you'd like about the chemicals that he uses or how he grows his corn. We focus on *local* food so that you can know the farmer that grew your food. Ask, interact, don't just trust a label." It came off fairly smooth, I thought. And it should have, because I was back on script and had probably said that line 100 times that afternoon.

"If I contact Jeremy, it will only be to tell him he shouldn't be poisoning people with bacteria," she snapped.

She had the last word.

She reached into the freezer case to grab a bag of corn from an organic competitor—a national brand whose product had no doubt been sprayed with Bacillus Thuringiensis, fertilized with mineral nitrogen, and produced by people whose names she could never learn, much less visit. Nevertheless, she walked away feeling quite confident in her food choice.

As a consumer, she is not unique. Many people reading this account now would probably have made the same decision. Why? Because that corn was everything she thought it needed to be?

No. On the contrary. She chose that corn because it was *not* any of the things that she had been taught to fear.

Food Insecurity.

If you stopped ten people in the organic aisle at any supermarket—or ten people in a health food store, dietary supplement shop, or even at the local farmers market—and asked them why they were buying what they had in their hand, you might get eleven different opinions.

The ever-increasing diversity of food philosophies, diets, and advice that one encounters in food today is overwhelming. The volumes of new data, articles, studies, and expert-opinions being circulated are not leading to more certainty with regard to food. On the contrary, we're experiencing a national sense of food insecurity. Not the kind of food insecurity that threatens childhood hunger, food deserts, or empty store shelves. America suffers the kind of insecurity that comes with being unsure of oneself—unsure of the right decisions—while under an inescapable daily duty to make those decisions, buy something, eat it, and feed it to your children.

As Americans today, we are increasingly insecure about our food, even while our pantries are chock full of it.

An entire generation has now grown up in America under the scourge of this food insecurity. Like no other generation in the history of mankind, my own generation has never known a time when we didn't have to weigh our food choice in the balance of our health and safety. As early as I can remember: White or wheat? Butter or margarine? Corn syrup or cane sugar? Diet or regular?

Adding to the problem is the fact that, to each of these seemingly trivial questions, we've been handed an equally trivial answer by an expert somewhere along the way. Only to have that answer contradicted some months or years later, of course.

The net effect is a growing anxiety—that insecurity—and a sense that whatever answer we are handed next probably won't be right in the end.

The most recent of these answers has come in the form of a small, circular emblem called the Organic label. It purports to solve all the insecurity you feel about a food choice by "certifying" that has been produced safely. But rest [un]assured: The organic label, too, will fail to end our quest for food security.

In this book, I am going to validate all your fears. I will assure you, the insecurity you sense is well-founded. The food you are likely snacking on right now is almost certainly not poisonous, but at the same time probably not wholesome, either.

I will validate your fears by getting to the root of the problem. No solutions can be reached until the actual problem is diagnosed. That must be our first aim.

The problem is, I am sorry to report, much deeper than just pesticides on your fruit or artificial ingredients in your food. If it were that superficial, the answers would be obvious, if not even easy.

For most of the last century, however, America has not just grown food with the wrong chemicals. We have fundamentally misunderstood food. We've misunderstood how it's made, what role it plays in our lives, and what we should hope to get from it.

It's time to understand food, again.

Once we understand food, we'll begin to see why local food offers such hope for America's future. Not just any old food from somewhere nearby, of course. No. As we understand food, we'll understand what makes local food truly local.

On the Contrary

Americans today buy foods that are non-this, free-of-that, and where none of the other is used. In the industry, it's known as "absence labeling"—declaring what's absent in the food instead of what's present. We are trained to read labels for non-GMO, pesticide-free, and no artificial hormones. Even the affirmative "organic" claim is primarily validated by a checklist of forbidden practices.

We are, quite simply, food contrarians.

The overwhelming sense in food today is to be against something. We are against chemicals. We are against antibiotics. We are against concentrated animal feeding operations (CAFO's). We are against genetically modified organisms (GMO's). And we are even against entire entities like Monsanto or Wal-Mart, to name a few.

Even local food falls squarely into this trap. In most attempts to define local foods, we find contrarian culture prevailing. We are against food miles. We are against out-of-season produce. We are against imported meat. We are against auction-buyers posing as food producers in our friendly, neighborhood farmers markets.

Even if food falls within one's local geography, the old contrarian maxims still prevail. After all, a local food enthusiast living next door to a CAFO is not interested in buying a hog from that neighbor, local as he may be.

For a whole generation, American consumers have been reacting against some perceived flaw in the food. From farmers markets to national organic brands, shoppers have been grasping for something *else*. It's not enough, it would seem, for food to be food. It must also carry assurances that it is not poisonous, cancer-causing, inhumanely raised or unjustly imported.

Local food is no different. It, too, is a reaction. It is a counter-cultural movement, and proud of it.

But counter to what?

The Health Food Craze.

At first, it was nutrition. Above all else, food ought to nourish our bodies and bring the building-blocks we need to fuel our growth and maintain health. But by the 1980's, there was a growing awareness that our food was failing us in this regard.

the American diet had become dominated by processed foods—high in preservatives, new formulations of fat, and new sources of sweeteners. Designed for shelf life and ease-of-use, food products catered to the fast-paced lifestyle of the post-war era. Gradually, over the course of decades, those adaptations came at the cost of food's nutrition value.

How did we let that happen? Significant shifts in the American economy coupled with changing social mores played a major role.

Rosie the Riveter meant the advent of dual income homes. And, dual incomes meant unprecedented amounts of discretionary income. Conceivably, America should have been able to afford the most nutritious, healthy food that the global market could offer. But quite the opposite resulted.

While dual income homes could have afforded the highest quality food, they had no spare time to prepare it. The end of home-making meant an unprecedented lack of time to prepare meals. Dinner once was an all afternoon production. But when both heads of household spend the afternoon at the office, and neither one in the kitchen, families turned to convenient alternatives. All of that discretionary income was directed at food options that valued convenience over quality.

The American menu changed significantly in the three decades that followed World War II. And, although it all happened so gradually, once America finally noticed the state our food was in, we reacted quite suddenly.

The health food craze that began in the 1980's and gained momentum throughout the 1990's was the first major reaction in food. In mass, America reacted to the menu changes that had been building for decades.

Claims like low sodium, fat-free, and heart-healthy seemed to dominate the food landscape overnight. People started counting calories, grams of this, and milligrams of that. Even the morning news was forever changed. To the staple segments of traffic, weather, and sports, news stations across the country added a health segments to their programming. Dieticians, chefs, and other food gurus were regular guests on every major network. Entire cooking channels emerged.

A normal day in the life of an American adult might include your morning weather report followed by a two-minute segment on how to read a nutrition label, all while eating your low-sodium breakfast cereal. Students of the 80's would spend more time learning to read a nutrition label and memorize the food pyramid than learning to plant a garden or cook a meal.

It was 1981 when Lean Cuisine, the healthy alternative to other frozen meals and "tv dinners," entered the food scene. The very next year, Coca-Cola introduced Diet Coke—the company's first variation in the Coke brand since it began in 1886. Jenny Craig was launched in 1983 and would grow to over 200 locations worldwide before the decade was through.

While these health foods dominated the grocery aisles through the 1980's, the fact remained that they were still processed foods. As the health food movement evolved, influencers like Oprah Winfrey began to popularize a new trend in healthy eating: fresh foods.

After her head-turning weight loss in 1988, which Winfrey later admitted was pure starvation, the television host gained back all her weight. Nine years later, though, Winfrey introduced a new diet from trainer Bob Greene. Unlike other contemporary diets that the likes of Jenny Craig had popularized, Winfrey and Greene featured fresh produce and meats, not low-this or free-of-that foods.

Gradually the realization spread that processed foods—even so-deemed "healthy" processed foods—needed to be avoided altogether. Buy flour, not baking mix. Eat apples, not apple sauce. Get a fresh cut of meat and a head of broccoli, not a frozen dinner.

But that's when we discovered something far more insidious than trans-fats and nitrates: Fresh food had been corrupted, too.

The Organic Food Movement.

By the mid-1990's, America was deeply engrossed in the mission to eat healthier. That pursuit left us looking first for health-claims on familiar processed foods. But soon, consumers learned that eating fresh, whole foods was healthier than a low-fat or reduced-sodium TV dinner.

Then came the real bad news. Word began to spread that fruits and vegetables—the very "healthy" foods that people were turning to—carried chemical residue on their surfaces. You might buy fresh meats to avoid nitrates, only to discover that the animal had been raised with a steady regimen of antibiotics. Your milk contains significant amounts of hormones. And simple leafy-green lettuce might have a contaminant called "E. Coli" which, at one time, could only be contracted from fecal matter. Indeed, it still only could come from fecal matter. But now, manure was being spread on lettuce fields in such concentrations that the lettuce could be fecal contaminated.

So, once again, America reacted. The second major food reaction was the organic movement of the late 90's and 2000's.

A new set of claims flooded the supermarket. Foods began to bear the labels natural, pure, and of course, organic. Animal products like meat, dairy, and eggs were advertised to be hormone and antibiotic free. Produce was heralded as chemical free. And while food brands still haven't come up with a good "poop-free" badge for their lettuce, in nearly every other respect the food industry sought ways to assure consumers that its products are safe and healthy to eat.

Enter the "organic" label.

An otherwise small and obscure farming movement, organic farming, suddenly found itself thrust into the limelight in the 1990's. Food retailers sought products that would meet the growing consumer demand for purity, and one group's practices garnered newfound attention. Organic farming had been around since the 1940's—itself a reaction against the chemical-laden farming that these prescient farmers foresaw as problematic more than a half-century before the consumer craze caught on. But for 50 years, *Organic Farming and Gardening* magazine—the bible of organic farming—was lumped in the same category with UFO testimonies and conspiracy theories.

Thrust into the mainstream seemingly overnight, however, the FDA developed an angst to clarify food claims. As the term began to show up on all manner of product, the FDA began to consider: What does "organic" really mean? Congress hurriedly passed a law, the Organic Foods Protection Act, and tasked the USDA with defining what farming practices could, and could not, be labeled as "organic."

Those rules went into effect in 2002, along with a federal program for certifying any producer who wished to use the term "organic" on their food labels. The rules provided clarity in an otherwise confusing storm of claims—natural, pure, and the like.

Rules, however, tend to emphasize rule-following. Whereas organic farming had grown to popularity as a method and philosophy around producing food, today the word "organic" is synonymous, not with certain growing methods, but with a federally-awarded certification. It is a certification, sadly, for which the qualifications only loosely approximate the original philosophy that began the movement so long ago.

Today, thanks to lobbying efforts by large chemical manufacturers, over 40 synthetic chemicals are permitted to be used in the production of foods without disqualifying them from using the "organic" label.[1]

While organic food sales continue to increase even today, that growth comes in large part because of the label becoming mainstream—almost ubiquitous—in conventional grocery stores. It had been a food label once relegated to health food stores and exclusively organic grocers—Whole Foods, for example. Today, consumers expect to find the organic label on products in any grocery store.

But for those conscientious consumers—the ones who have been on the leading edge of both the health food and the organic food movements—confidence in the organic claim is waning.

The Local Reaction.

Today, after decades of reacting, a new question has made its way into the food consumer's mind. Not "what's in it?" And not even, "How was it grown?" But consumers today are asking a new question that the food industry is ill equipped to answer: Where did it come from?

In addition to the increasing inclusion of non-organic inputs permitted for so-labeled "organic" foods, another confidence killer has been the increase in imported organics. Even if one does trust the US Department of Agriculture's certifying process, it's quite another matter to trust the certification process in the developing nations eager to sell their products to the U.S. markets. A 2017 audit by the USDA found that nearly $2 billion of America's organic food is imported, and the inspector general couldn't confirm that food labeled as organic was, in fact, grown organically in its country of origin.[2]

A research agency, The Hartman Group, has been charting the natural and organics market each year since its rise to popularity over a decade ago. In their most recent report, they rattled grocery marketers by reporting, "Organic's and natural's halos of health and authenticity have lost some of their luster," adding that, "*Local* is emerging as a category poised to surpass both organic and natural."[3]

But ask a consumer to define local, and they might struggle. Ask why they buy local and you will get a myriad of reasons. The reaction is not a well-defined movement.

Why? Because it's still not clear to everyone what they are reacting against.

Health food emerged as a reaction to a clear set of ingredients and components that were found to be unhealthy. Organic food emerged as a reaction to a clear set of farming practices and inputs that were found to be unnatural.

Local food is now emerging as a reaction to what, exactly? A clear number of miles that have been found to be too far? No. There is not even a consensus on what distance qualifies as local.

Before we can understand what local food is, we must understand what it is against. We must clearly identify and fully understand that which local food is in reaction to.

What the health food and organic food movements reacted against were mere symptoms—byproducts of a food system that produced artificial and unnatural foods. But the root issue—the real "thing" against which conscientious food consumers have been resisting— is not any one symptom or quality of our food. Those were the ripples we noticed first. The epicenter dates back nearly a century, to a radically new way that we began creating food in America in the 20th century.

We are reacting against *Industrial Food*.

Consumer ~~Goods~~ Foods

When I was born in 1983, my parents took me home from the hospital to the 80-acre farm that I would call home for the next 18 years. It was the same family farm that my father had lived on his entire life. And, it was the same farm that my grandfather had bought in 1941. From the kitchen window on that farm I could see my great-grandfather's old farmhouse down the street.

In my childhood, that farm produced a litany of crops. Yes, corn and soybeans were on the list. But I also remember growing wheat and barley, which both yielded straw for livestock bedding. We raised beef cattle, dairy cattle, hogs, and ducks. We grew and bailed alfalfa hay every summer to feed our livestock.

By my 18th birthday, however, that diversity of crops had dwindled down to just corn and soybeans.

The livestock pens were empty. A few old, unused bales of straw rotted in the dilapidated barn. Grain was our specialty now.

In less than two decades, the business of farming had changed. It was more streamlined, efficient, and more productive. Farms became specialized, and with specialization came efficiency. On one farm like ours, we no longer grew the grain and fed it to the livestock. Instead, we specialized in grain. We grew corn and soy beans, and we grew more of them than we ever had before.

Genetic hybrid enhancements, newer techniques, and better fertilizers meant that yields were at all-time highs. Bigger equipment, mechanization, and smart technologies meant that one farmer could grow and sell more grain himself than the large families who worked together a generation ago.

Farming was simpler, too. All we had to do was send the grain down the "assembly line" of farming to the next station. There it could become food for you, fuel for your cars, and one of a thousand different synthesized products. Or, most commonly, it would be fed to cattle, hogs, and poultry just like the livestock that we once had. Except now, livestock ate our grain on a different farm—a farm specializing in cattle, or hogs, or chicken.

It was brilliant. It was booming. It was industrial.

The year I turned 18, I left the farm for good. I was off to find a career that would never include farming (or, so I thought). Not because I was disinterested, but because this new way of farming was so efficient that it no longer needed me.

But, why? How could a once-bustling farm become an enterprise that didn't have a use for its own residents? Because food had become just another consumer good.

Immediately following World War II, American progress was booming in nearly every respect. Manufacturing was roaring.

Consumer spending was high. The GI Bill meant people needed houses in droves—and not tiny apartments in the city. The typical American family wanted a suburban lot with a garage, a state-of-the-art kitchen, a television, two-and-a-half children and a car. And in the post-war, economy, more families than ever could afford all of that, too.

All seemed right in the world.

We had entered the war as an energetic young nation just awakening from the Great Depression. We exited the war running full-steam ahead with an eye-opening perspective on what our young nation was truly capable of. During the war, we had mobilized manufacturing and production like never before—all for the war effort.

With no enemies to fight, however, it was time to turn every industrious bullet factory and war-plane assembly line back into civilian uses. Armed with the knowledge of what real productivity looked like when life depended on it, factories began churning out more consumer goods, automobiles, and yes, food than ever before.

Manufacturing output was not the only byproduct of the war, though. Imagine feeding millions of troops on three continents thousands of miles from home. Our military perfected logistics, warehousing, distribution, and even food preservation. Canned meats, powdered dairy, individually wrapped portions of products as inane as salt and pepper were not only imagined, but created, used, and perfected in the 44 short months that America warred with Germany and Japan.

Within 10 years, those achievements in food distribution which had led us to victory in Europe, would lead to a total transformation of the American cupboard and kitchen. Now that we had discovered how to ship, store, and distribute entire meals that required no refrigeration and could be unwrapped and eaten in minutes—it didn't matter whether we were feeding soldiers in a foxhole from the commissary, or feeding a family in the suburbs from the supermarket. This was how America would eat for more than a generation.

So, the origins of that first great reaction—the health food movement—began as early as the 1940's. It was then that food became a manufactured good. It would be 50 years before America reacted against that decision.

Agriculture was not untouched, either. Splitting an atom means a waterfall effect of scientific discovery. Even smaller scale explosions required tremendous chemistry productions. When you drop more than six billion pounds of TNT on your enemy in four years, you become quite industrious at manufacturing it. The premier ingredient in TNT is, of course, the "N"—Nitrogen—which also happens to be a quintessential fertilizer.

It was 1943, nearing the end of the war, when researchers at the Mississippi Agricultural Experiment Station came up with a way of injecting nitrogen in a liquid form directly into soils.[4] The amount of corn that we expected to harvest per acre when I was a kid on the farm had increased six-fold since my grandfather first bought those acres in 1941. Those gains were due in no small part to America's ability to manufacture and apply Nitrogen in massive quantities, first in bombs, then in fertilizer. The basic industrial process was the same for producing both nitrogen bombs and nitrogen fertilizer.

So, the origins of that second great reaction—the organic food movement—were laid in the 1940's, as well. As soon as chemically-driven farming began, there were dissenters. It wouldn't be until the 1990's that those dissenters would become mainstream under the "organic" moniker.

Even so, the dissent was then and is today misguided. Proponents of organic farming fail to see that chemical-laden farming practice is not the root problem itself. Relying heavily on chemicals in farming is merely a symptom of a greater fallacy that has befallen America. Artificial, preservative-laden foods are merely the logical outcome of a fundamentally flawed philosophy on food production. They are the down-stream effects from the watershed moment when America industrialized its food system in the post-war era.

We industrialized food as an unconscious choice, a sort of unwitting decision to esteem food as just another consumer good—no different than a pair of shoes or a color television set.

And why not? We can manufacture both products, food and consumer goods alike. Why not apply industrial manufacturing advancements to our food as we have done electronics, clothes, and cars?

The difference is that nature, given the opportunity, can manufacture food without us. While there is no natural process by which a color television emerges from the ground, the same cannot be said of a cucumber. Industry is required to create televisions. But there is an important truth that would take America almost a century to realize: Industry is not only unnecessary, it's quite possibly detrimental to the manufacture of food.

Food as a Weapon

One war gave way to another, and another. By the 1970's America was embroiled in an altogether different kind of war than the one it had fought with Nazi Germany and Imperial Japan. The Cold War needed no advancements in food preservation or distribution. But it would bring altogether different changes to our food.

Whereas the Second World War taught us how to make each farm a more productive version of itself, the Cold War that followed would thrust American farming into a completely new industrial age. Industrialization applied to a farm makes that farm more productive. But when industrialization is applied to farming at large—to an entire realm that was collectively American farming— then each farm is transformed into something quite different than it had been. Each farm ceases to be a whole farm in and of itself, and instead becomes a contributor to the industrial farming complex.

The Cold War had America looking for ways that it could defeat its enemy, the Soviet Union, in just about any way other than a battlefield. This war was fought without a weapon. Shots were fired not with guns but with speech, ideas, and propaganda. And the biggest shots—the bombs dropped, if you will—were economic shots.

Choking off supplies of one product or flooding markets with another were attacks intended to topple the Russian economy, not it's armaments. Many Americans recall vividly the gas shortages of the 1970's. But few outside the farming community have ever realized how America's agricultural exports were weaponized for the war.

Secretary of Agriculture, Earl Butz, saw America's prairieland—that great expanse of Midwestern soil—as our equivalent to the Soviet oil fields. In the global markets, the Soviets had oil. America had food. And with emerging economies around the world needing food just as much as they needed petroleum, Butz hatched a plan to make sure whenever those nations needed food, it would be American agricultural products that they imported.

"Food is a weapon," Butz famously stated. To wield it, however, Butz needed to increase America's productivity in agriculture by orders of magnitude. We couldn't merely increase output by incremental gains, but by exponential multipliers. He needed to change more than just how productive farmers could be, he needed to change how productivity was achieved.

Butz would have to transform the concept of an American farmer. But, short of nationalizing the farming industry, how could one government agency transform the very idea of what it meant to be a farmer? The USDA could not send armed forces to seize control and operation of America's farmland. Butz had a huge challenge ahead of him: He had to convince the American farmer to fundamentally transform, and to do it at his own expense.

You see, we were fighting for freedom. It was the communists, not us freedom-loving Americans, who centralized power. The fascist, not the land-of-the-free, oppressed the poor. The Dictators, not the beacon of democracy, seized control over all means of production.

How could Earl Butz rally the American farmers who owned and controlled this treasure trove of a natural resource he so ingeniously sought to mobilize? How could he recruit them into this war, to transform their own hereditary farms, and redefine the very vocation of farming that defined their identity for generations?

He gave them a mission: Feed the world.

He gave them a vision: Farm fencerow to fencerow.

He gave them a challenge: Get big or get out.

And it worked.

The world I was born into was already nearly a decade into this mission, and momentum was building. I still vividly remember playing our part in America's grand calling to feed the world. We spent our winters chopping down fence rows. Neighbors cleared entire patches of forest, buried trees, burnt stumps, and got ready to plow a few more acres the following year.

The versatile chore tractor that was the centerpiece of the industrial farm since that post-WWII explosion was now obsolete. No farmer needed a single implement that could grind feed, mow pastures, and plant corn all in one. Instead, he needed a monolithic machine that, while far less versatile, could do one thing with unthinkable force: cultivate grain.

Or, conversely, on farms that weren't as well suited for the grain specialty as ours, livestock became the monolith. The same rule applied: get big or get out. Big barns, automated feeders, and huge herds that began to arrive by the truck load—the semi-truck kind, not the pickup.

All this would cost a considerable amount of money, of course. A versatile tractor in the 40's cost a few thousand dollars at most. A combine harvester in the 70's could cost a hundred thousand or more. How could the farmers afford such a capital investment?

Unfortunately for farmers, the capital became all too available. Banks were more than eager to lend the capital on USDA-guaranteed loans. When the borrower's own credit and collateral would hardly justify millions in farm investment, the risk was underwritten by government backing.

Sound familiar? The 2008 mortgage crisis was not the first time that we faced economic uncertainty due to government-backed loan programs. The financial crisis for farms in the 1980's was so grave that suicide rates among farmers were nearly double the national average.[5] Farmers were declaring bankruptcy at record rates, losing the land their forefathers had left to them, and all for the cause of a war that they never enlisted for.

In 1970, the average American farm held just $80,900 in debt. By 1980, that number had more-than-doubled to $168,000 per farm.[6] In that same time, over 200,000 farms ceased to exist. When one farm declared bankruptcy, their lands were absorbed into the next larger farm still holding on.[7] Farms got progressively larger, but all that land required still more equipment to keep up. More equipment meant more debt, and the cycle continues even to the present day.

Today, there are one-quarter fewer farms in America as there were in 1970, yet they farm roughly the same number of acres. Farms are fewer. Farms are larger. And altogether they export 60 percent of the world's grain.[8] Earl Butz' plan to turn the American farmers into a cohesive, federally-orchestrated economic army worked all too perfectly. But the casualties would take decades to realize.

Industrial Food

The term local food is a reaction. Just as health food was a reaction against heavily processed foods, and organic foods were a reaction against chemically-tainted foods, in the same way local food is a reaction against the overarching American food and farming trends that made those chemicals and manufacturing processes a part of our food supply to begin with.

In the previous chapters, we've explored the trajectory from World War II through the Cold War which fundamentally transformed our nation's farms and, consequently, our food. Today, the term that is most commonly used to describe that trajectory, and the systems that it fostered, has been *Industrial Food*.

Local food is a reaction against industrial food.

But, outside of the history which we've recounted, how can we define industrial food? If we are to understand what local food really is, we must first learn to identify industrial food for the traits that make it objectionable.

There are three key characteristics to industrial food. They are the same characteristics of anything industrial, really, be it car manufacturing, clothing, or otherwise. To produce a good in an industrial fashion, it's production must follow these three characteristics: 1) **specialized tasks**, applied in 2) **repeatable processes**, which allow for 3) **scalable growth**.

Earl Butz understood this truth. He envisioned a farming system which specialized farms, gave them cookie-cutter practices that could be applied on any farm with similar outcomes, and it enabled his economic army to grow to epic proportions. Most insidious of all, he attained a nearly unanimous buy-in among farmers adopting his mission. Adherents were so passionate about their newfound call to "feed the world" that they were willing to take on the costs of executing this elaborate industry themselves in order to achieve the collective mission as their dutiful service to their nation.

In some respects, Butz' achievements are some of the most effective examples of policy enactment in American history. He accomplished precisely what he set out to accomplish, and he did it all with policy instead of nationalized, coerced control. It's a textbook policy case.

As farms specialized, they did it willingly and eagerly. Some farms specialized in grain production. Others divested of lands and invested in large barns and mechanized livestock operations instead. Others still left farming altogether, opting instead for careers in "agronomy"—a new specialty involving laboratory soil testing, seed hybridization, animal nutrition studies, and the like.

Regardless which specialization any farm pursued within the newly nationalized industry of farming, the impact for farmers and food consumers was the same. For farmers, no single farm would be able to create food using their own resources—growing their grain that they feed to their own animals which they had bred from their own herd genetics. So-called "finishing farms" would buy young livestock from specialized breeders, and feed from yet a different supplier.

To the food consumer, this specialization means that a shopper can no longer know and appreciate where their food comes from, because it comes from myriad contributors in an anonymized system. Specialization of the farming inputs makes nameless, faceless food in the supermarket aisle.

Next, devising repeatable processes for those specialized farms to follow was not quite so simple. Creating a grain program, for example, that could be applied on soils from Northern Minnesota to southern Kansas and get the same results—despite varying soil profiles, climate, and sunlight hours—sounded impossible at first.

But just as some livestock farms began to specialize in breed stock, so, too, would grain farms begin to specialize in seed production.

Specialized seed farmers began to focus entirely, not on producing grain itself, but on developing hybridized seeds that yet another specialized farm buy, plant, and reap a harvest using. Seeds were developed especially suited to each environment. By selectively breeding one variety that could endure droughts in Kansas and breeding another variety that could endure cold soils in Minnesota, the seed industry enabled farmers in every region enlist in the USDA's veritable grain army.

Every grain farm shifted its focus from an approach which asked, "what grain is my soil most suited to produce, and does my own farm—livestock—most need?" to instead asking, "what grain can I produce in the highest volumes?" The answer, it turned out, would be corn, corn, a little soybean, and then more corn. Which, in turn, affected how livestock farms chose to standardize as well.

The livestock industry found that there was little point in toiling with once-popular meats which could not be raised on corn and soy alone. Rabbits, for example, were once favored over chicken in many American kitchens. But they require a complex ration of roughage. Contrast that with the Cornish Cross hen—which could convert less than twelve pounds of corn and soy grain into four pounds of meat in under eight weeks. Today, very few American consumers even recognize rabbit as a meat, much less have prepared or eaten it.

No longer would farmers need to use their own ingenuity and adaptability to find the best grain to grow on their particular soils in their particular climate. Then, further experiment to find the best breed of livestock that could convert that grain—be it corn, or barley, or wheat, or spelt, or oats—into meat while also thriving in their climate's seasonality, temperatures, and other factors.

No, all that know-how was obsolete in the age of Industrial agriculture. Today, nearly every one of the nine billion chickens slaughtered in America's industrial food system are Cornish Cross breeds, raised in nearly identical barns, fed identical feed, for precisely 42 days—no more, no less—regardless of the weather outside.

Pork has industrialized in much the same way around a few select breeds. The hog breeds were chosen not only for their own feed conversion traits, but also for their breed's ability to endure confined conditions. Most hogs, when penned up in close quarters with other hogs, resort to chewing each other's ears and tails off. Breeds were favored who could endure such conditions without the adverse behavior reactions. Just in case, though, piglets routinely had their teeth and tails removed soon after birth to avoid gruesome casualties later into adolescence.

Beef is the industry that's still the most diverse in genetics, due in large part to the simple fact that cattle take longer to reproduce.

One cow gives birth to one calf after a 9-month gestation, of which there have been hardly 100 generations since World War II. Meanwhile, chicken breeders have been able to experiment with thousands of generations of offspring in that span.

Altogether, this grain-to-feed-to-meat "factory" that America has become is quite splendidly industrialized. Farms are specialized. Processes, and their expected outcomes, are repeatable in every respect. As a result, this farming system has attained unprecedented scale.

Three species of livestock lent themselves to repeatable outcomes: beef, pork, and chicken. Today, 92 percent of America's meat diet consists of one of these three species. Most Americans have never tasted rabbit, quail, pheasant, guinea, goat, or lamb—the menagerie of meats that any butcher shop would have offered at the turn of last century.

Wheat is the overwhelming flour of choice. Oats, barley, and rye are all but forgotten grains in our diet. A staggering number of foods on grocery shelves have additives and sweeteners made almost entirely from corn. Nearly all our cooking oils are derived from soy, or it's cousin, canola.

Corn, soy, wheat, beef, pork, and chicken could be called the six major food groups of the American diet. Even the fruits and vegetables we enjoy today come in such a limited variety that the produce section of any supermarket—brightly lit and an ostensible cornucopia—would pale in comparison to the produce markets that our grandparents once shopped.

But America is hungry for something different.

Dehumanized Food

There's another word for specialization. It's an agricultural word.
It's called monoculture—the practice of growing, or "cultivating,"
just one crop. And while it's true that most row-crop farmers grow
at least two crops: corn, possibly wheat, and soy beans. That itself
is a far cry from the cornucopia that farmers once produced.
When you consider industrial livestock producers, however, the
term monoculture is painfully accurate.

And there is a link between farming and food. That statement
sounds obvious, but many have failed to make the connection
cognitively. As our food production has become more and more
monocultural, our food has become more monolithic. Industrial
food, for all its efficiencies, offers the American consumer today a
more limited diet than the diverse farming enterprises provided for
generations before World War II. What options remain are

increasingly dependent on a short list of ingredients like corn, soy, and wheat.

The cumulative effect of this monocultural industrial food system is that we are now eating a diet in America today that is anthropologically unique. That is to say: We are eating now like no human population has eaten in the history of mankind. Is that bad? Well, we aren't sure. And that is bad.

The ramifications of eating the way we uniquely eat now in America are simply not yet known. Anecdotally, our change in diet is correlated with increased food allergies and sensitivities. There exist today a host of chronic illnesses like colitis, Crohn's, and diabetes—conditions that were once rare in the human population, now commonplace.

Even so, it is not the biological ramifications of industrial foods that are the most concerning. After all, health hazards have plagued every industrialized system, and industrial solutions abound. Factories, for example, were once plagued with workplace injuries. Machine design was adapted to be less dangerous. Air pollution once affected every industrialized city, but emission controls and air cleaners have brought about tremendous reversal of those ill effects.

The same is happening in industrialized food. Industrial answers abound for industrial problems. Is your body deficient in nutrients? Take this new supplement. Is the soil degrading? Apply this new fertilizer. Is the soil eroding away entirely with increased tillage? Apply for one of the new cover-crop programs. Don't forget to terminate those cover crops each spring with a chemical herbicide like glyphosate before planting your crops again.

The two recent reactions in modern food—the health food movement, and the organic food movement—have both been industrial answers to industrial problems. Replacing artificial ingredients with natural ones, all the while still mass-producing foods sourced from monocultural farms, is still an industrial answer. Replacing synthetic chemicals with organic chemicals even as you apply those organic chemicals to thousands of contiguous acres of corn and soybeans—the crop from which is bound for a concentrated animal feeding operation with hundreds of thousands of so-called organically raised livestock under one roof—is an industrial solution to a consumer perception problem.

Neither health food nor organic food address the underlying issue at the foundation of industrial food—the very industrial nature, the industrial approach, and the industrial philosophies that led America to reinvent how food was made.

What is it about an industrial system of food that makes an unredeemable and incurable dilemma? The problem is that an industrial system is, inherently, a dehumanizing system.

There is no crop program, spray, or pill that can restore dignity to people in a system that treats them as less than human.

The Factory is Dehumanizing

Vast expanses of fields are the factory of our food, and those factories are as dehumanizing for farmers today as a twelve-hour shift in a smoke-filled iron forge at the turn of the last century.

It's dehumanizing to reduce food production to mere mineral mining.

A mine—that's all that a field of grain amounts to today. And for a vocation that has passed along the art of producing food from the earth for generations, it's a dehumanizing evolution to exchange that noble profession in order to join the ranks of Earl Butz' army as a mineral extractor, no longer a producer of food.

Farmers no longer feed America. They feed an industry—an industry focused more on the global export market than the domestic food needs, at that.

It's dehumanizing to the farmer who deposits a lab-engineered mining device each spring into the fields where his father once produced food. A farmer now deposits a mining device in the shape of a seed. It sends tiny drills—roots—deep down into the earth to extract valuable elements. Carbon, hydrogen, and minerals are pulled up and stored in a capsule—a kernel—at a height that a machine can easily retrieve them. And that's where this farmer's contribution to America's diet ends. Today's American farmer produces an industrial commodity, like coal or iron ore, and sends it down the assembly line.

The elements that he mined are arranged in transportable form, not unlike an ingot of iron. Fats, proteins, and starches all held together in a non-perishable granule that can flow like liquid through augers and bins. All of this makes it easily stored and easily transported to the factories where the minerals can be reassembled into forms that people like you and I might recognize as food.

Juices, yogurts, salad dressings, and a host of other foods you might have classified as "natural" are all sweetened with corn syrup. Soy shows up in nearly every product requiring oil— including bread—and is the primary ingredient in most protein alternatives or dairy replacements.

But a large portion of these grains are not converted to food at a factory using machines and mixers. It's an altogether different kind of factory that converts a full third of America's grain into food. Meat, to be exact. And the machines powering those factories all have eyes, ears, and tails—that is, if their pen-mates haven't chewed theirs off yet.

Here again, the factory is dehumanizing.

Among the knowledge that this vocation once relied on, fathers once taught their sons to care for an animal's well-being, and to care for the soil's well-being by integrating livestock with crops in harmony. But those farmers who no longer grow grain—or mine the fields, as it were—have exchanged their hereditary vocation for yet another dehumanizing industrial role.

Gone is the art of animal husbandry. Farmers today needn't learn the impacts of weather, diet, seasons, and even breeding traits on their herds. The weather is always ideal for growing in the climate-controlled barns. Driven by efficiency, industry leaders like Tyson and Smithfield have prescribed the exact breeds of livestock and diet to use—even supplying both the animals and the feed to the grower for them to use.

This is a fact that cannot be understated: It's also dehumanizing to be inhumane toward other creatures.

When regular chores on the so-called "farm" include hauling out the dead—a mere statistically-predictable casualty of the large-scale production—that is a dehumanizing existence. On today's livestock factories, the lives lost are accounted for in just the same way that you would account for broken glass in a stemware factory. But that's not how any generation of farmer that came before us thought.

It's no surprise, then, that a growing number of farmers are looking for an alternative. For all their purported benefit to the consumer, the natural food movement and the organic certification program have brought no relief to the farmers. Producing organically-certified corn that goes into organically-certified beef, pork, or chicken is no more dignified a process than industrial farming was before the organic program began. Organic livestock is raised under equally inhumane conditions as conventional, and the industry for producing them is equally as dehumanizing to the farmer.

Fortunately for these farmers, they aren't the only ones hungry for a change.

The Grocery Store is Dehumanizing

Grab a cart. It's time to become a warehouse picker for the next hour. Or, didn't you realize that's the job for which you had volunteered? Grocery stores ingeniously figured out a way to get their customers to do one of the most tedious tasks in the goods distribution business: picking. Tedious tasks are one of the most difficult to hire people to do. Why? Because, tedious tasks are— you guessed it—dehumanizing.

Recruiting you, however, was easy. All they had to do was add a little better lighting, make their aisle markers more aesthetically pleasing, and suddenly they turned labor-intensive retail into a 100,000-square-foot warehouse that could be operated on a skeleton crew. That is, of course, if you don't count all those "workers" pushing their carts in the head-count.

This was possibly the single most significant enhancement that our post-war-era grocery industry made upon its precursor, the wartime food logistics system. In the commissary, there would have been one unlucky enlisted man assigned to picking duty. In the supermarket, you've been drafted.

Of course, picking and packing your own cart isn't such a bad trade if it serves to keep prices down. Cost-conscious shoppers might even appreciate trading a little of their time for lower prices. It's not only what takes place in these aisles that's dehumanizing, it's also what doesn't go on. When we gave up talking to our neighborhood grocer across the counter in exchange for picking our products out of a well-lit warehouse ourselves, we also gave up a human connection to our food.

Have a question about the ingredients? Read the label. Have a question about how to cook it? Read the label. Want to know if it's any good or not? Of course it is, why, just look at those claims on the package!

And, as you're tasked with determining this food's fitness for your family without any shred of human interaction, the data provided is even more degrading. You are more than the proper ratios of carbohydrates, proteins, fats, and a small handful of vitamins and minerals.

The nutrition facts label has become so commonplace within the span of just one generation that nobody has stopped to consider its sociological undertones. Can a tiny table in seven-point, Arial font tell a mother whether a certain food is fit for her family?

Apparently so. Reading nutrition labels has been a core part of school curriculums for America's youth for two decades now. But I want you to consider how dehumanizing it is to reduce the American food consumer to just a dozen or so measurements. Eat enough of this, and not too much of that, and you will be adequately fed?

This is, unfortunately, a perfectly logical expression of an industrial food supply. A deconstruction of the human experience of food that outputs predictably repeatable foods that can be purchased with a predictably repeatable rubric. Compare line seven of this table to line seven of the competitor's table to determine which of these products is a better choice for you and your family.

Sound like a natural human process? It is most definitely not. It's unnatural, unflattering, and decidedly dehumanizing.

You can trust me. I swear.

By the first century, it had become very customary for people in near-Eastern cultures to swear oaths. They were used to implore others to trust a statement or a testimony. The greater the thing sworn by, the more trustworthy the statement was.

It's not a practice altogether unfamiliar to us today. "I swear by my grandma's bones," some might say. Or, even "I'll swear on a stack of Bibles." It's the idea that one person's word isn't enough to validate itself, but tack on an oath of some kind, and credibility increases.

For first-century Jews in New Testament times, it was their temple that held the highest esteem—not grandma's bones or a stack of Bibles. They placed their oaths on that temple. But that created a moral dilemma for the religious leaders of the day. The temple was, after all, a sacred place. It was considered irreverent to swear by the temple.

They had an ingenious solution, or so they thought. They would maintain an aura of reverence by swearing their oaths instead by the furnishings in the temple, not the temple itself. Of course, not everyone accepted this as a justifiable work-around. A debate raged about what venerable object one might swear by without being guilty of religious irreverence.

They brought this question to Jesus for him to weigh in. His response was not what they were looking for. He said to them: "Let your 'Yes' be 'Yes,' and your 'No,' 'No.'"[9]

In other words, if you must find some sacred thing you can swear by just to make people believe you, maybe reverence isn't your biggest problem. Maybe it's trust itself.

This is a timely lesson to remember today because one of the first things to erode in a dehumanizing system is trust. Simply put: America has lost trust in food.

According to the "2016 Food Revolution Study" from Chicago-based Label Insight, nearly all study respondents (94 percent) said that a food brands' transparency about product contents and production methods are important to them. That is not surprising at all. What is surprising is that 75 percent of those same respondents went on to report that they, in fact, do not trust the accuracy of food labels.[10] They need to feel confident in what they're being told about food, but as they browse the supermarket's industrial food offerings, they don't have that confidence.

That erosion of trust has led to a proliferation of oaths in food labeling. And many people are now asking which oath is to be trusted. Certified Organic or Certified All Natural? Is cage-free good, or is it free-range that matters, or must hens be pasture-raised? Which is more important: non-GMO or chemical-free? What makes for good beef: grass-fed or grass-finished?

As we walk down the aisle of a supermarket today asking ourselves which of the many "oaths" embossed on the front of the package we can trust, the best answer is the simple one. Just as Jesus answered, "let your 'yes' be 'yes,'" wouldn't it be a welcomed change if food were food? America is longing for a simpler time when food was food, meat was meat, and eggs were eggs.

When food today must have insignia, certifications, emblem on top of emblem all over your carton of eggs just to convince the consumer that they can eat it—it seems those industrial answers to food aren't working any more.

Oaths are a poor substitute for trust. Regulation is a poor substitute for transparency.

RE: Industrial Food

When America realized that it was eating unhealthy food, we reacted with a shift toward foods marketed as "healthy"—free of the feared fat, preservatives, and sodium. Years later, attention turned toward eating fresh foods instead of packaged ones. But America then realized that its fresh food supply was laden with pesticides, hormones, and antibiotics. We reacted once again, this time with a shift toward foods marketed as "natural" and eventually "organic."

Still the healthy, natural, and so-called organic foods continue to come from an industrial food system. So, where does America turn when we realize that we can trust neither the "healthy" claims nor the "organic" claims?

We go to the source. We see for ourselves. And we call it "local."

The phrase "local food" has become the most convenient moniker for the reaction against industrial food in America. Other names have been tried: slow food, sustainable food, and even "beyond organic." But time and again, the one term that is most frequently called upon to sum up the notion has been "local."

As summaries often do, however, the term "local food" over-simplifies the reaction.

To be sure, there is a strong bias in the local food movement for foods produced in proximity to one's physical location. But that is by no means an exhaustive definition. After all, a popular vendor in most American farmers markets is the local coffee roaster. It goes without saying, of course, that such vendors are selling an agricultural commodity that cannot be grown anywhere in the continental United States.

How can Columbian coffee be "local" in Indiana? Because "local" food is about more than just location. It has become a broadly applied moniker for a philosophy of buying food from a source that you can know, understand, and trust. Often that trust is garnered through simple geographic proximity. But there is also an overlap in purchasing behavior between truly geographically-local food, and foods identified in other measures of trust—measures such as fair-trade, source-identified, single-origin, sustainably-grown, and the list goes on.

Rather than the farm's geographic location with respect to the buyer, what resonates most with consumers of local food is the attribute of transparency—both in knowing the source of the food, but also in understanding its production methods.

Those production methods had been verifiable, or so we thought, by the "organic" label. But trust has eroded in the organic claim as its adulteration with chemical farming has come to light. As the

Hartman Group's report confirmed, "Organic's and natural's halos of health and authenticity have lost some of their luster."[2]

But local food is shining bright. Even though the food industry—which is decidedly industrial—has proved reluctant, at best, to give local food a seat at the table.

An "Organic" Movement

It is rather ironic that the local food movement has arisen more "organically" than did the actual organic food movement. Since its first publication in 1942, *Organic Farming and Gardening* magazine remained a fringe publication for nearly half a century. By the early 1990's, it's reach was still well under a million subscribers. By the time that its publisher altogether cancelled printing of the magazine in 2015, its readership had fallen to just over 300,000.[11]

It's true: The organic food label has soared to consumer popularity in recent decades. But only after federal rules were enacted in 2002 arising from the Organic Foods Protection Act. As late as 2012, there were still a mere 16,525 organic farms in America according to the United States Department of Agriculture census.

If that sounds like a large number of farms, consider this. There are over 18,000[12] community gardens providing local food to hyperlocal communities in the U.S. In 1994, there were less than 2,000 farmers markets in the nation. By 2013, the number of markets in the United States had more than quadrupled to 8,144 markets nationwide.[13] Estimates range from 100,000 to 200,000 farms are vending at those markets.

To put it all together, that means there are as many as 10 times the number of farms vending at local farmers markets as there are certified organic farms in America.

Add to that a proliferation of farm-to-table restaurants, where chefs assemble ever-changing menus of the seasonally-available foods from their local farms. Think further about the hundreds of farm cooperatives and aggregators nationwide, which help to put local producers on even-footing with the larger wholesale distributors, gaining placement of independent farmers' products on grocery store shelves.

Local food seems to have gained an unstoppable momentum.

But how? All of this growth in farmers markets, small farms, and farm-to-table systems has taken place without a central campaign. No act of Congress catalyzed the adoption of local food. And no unifying group or union binds local food purveyors together.

In fact, quite the opposite has been true. The federal government is America's largest customer. As the government's budget goes, so goes a large swath of American industry. Hospitals, schools, universities, military bases, and other institutions that receive government funding must also follow government purchasing practices. Namely, they are required to buy from the lowest bidder. In fact, the proximity of the bidder is not allowed to be considered as a qualitative differentiator. Industrially-produced foods from afar will underbid local food nearly every time.

The private sector is not much better. For three years, two co-founders and I struggled to grow a local food company by calling on retail grocery stores. We had invested significant capital into equipment, infrastructure, and inventory. That investment made it possible for us to offer local foods at market price. We were price competitive—even cheaper than national brands in some categories—with a higher-quality product produced from local farms identified on each bag.

Nevertheless, the company failed. Why? For one, the grocery industry simply could not find a way to buy our products. Too small to supply the entire Eastern half of the U.S., many distributors didn't see a point in carrying our products. And facing the immense pressure of shrinking margins in their own business, grocery stores couldn't afford the administrative hassle of adding a new vendor.

This trend is known as "vendor consolidation"—a business tactic for reducing overhead cost by, quite simply, writing fewer checks in larger amounts to a smaller selection of suppliers. We didn't make the cut.

Regulatory hurdles present yet another challenge for local producers. Ironically, ever since the organic rules were enacted in 2002, farmers have been unable to market their goods with the adjective "organic" unless they become certified by the USDA. Such a certification can entail thousands of dollars to cover the cost of third-party inspections, audits, and fees.

Outbreaks of foodborne illnesses have precipitated a litany of new rules. Such outbreaks are exclusively the byproduct of an industrial food system—never once has an endemic food illness originated from a small-scale, local farm. Nevertheless, the reactionary regulations are imposed indiscriminately on all producers, industrial farms and local farms alike. The former is unfazed by the regulations, while the latter is stifled greatly by the costs to maintain compliance in an ever-growing web of red tape surrounding food and farming.

The entrepreneurial farmers who venture into the local food scene do so at their own risk. No federal program markets their goods domestically like grains are marketed abroad. No subsidy to underwrite their risks exist as they do for industrial-scale farms. In fact, until very recently, crop insurance (a federally underwritten program) was not offered to producers of food crops like vegetables and fruits as it is to commodity grain producers.

The obstacles are significant, costly and daunting.

Despite all of this, and while institutional support for organic farming abounded, the penetration of local food products to the consumer market through alternative means—farmers markets, community supported agriculture programs, and the like—has doubled each decade for two straight decades. Today, the sheer volume of farms that are supplying their communities with local food eclipse organic farms by a factor of 10.

How?

All the things that impelled industrial food to completely transform America's diet—federal subsidy, technological advancement, propagandized farm philosophies, and a nationalist mission to feed the world—are not afforded to local food. Its conception and development have run entirely counter to these forces.

On the contrary, local food has risen to popularity despite all odds. Local food has truly grown organically. It is truly a grass-roots movement.

Food Independence

In a small, provincial government building in Philadelphia in 1776, 56 men committed treason against their king by affixing their signatures to a declaration of America's independence. But many of those signers had not always been eager for revolt. In the years leading up to America's revolution, founding fathers like Benjamin Franklin and John Hancock, and others like them, tried earnestly to restore the colonies to the monarch with diplomacy and reforms.

So how did they end up traitors and rebels? Because in the end, it was the very nature of a monarch's relationship to its colonies that made reforms inadequate to satisfy America's needs. Colonists were not seeking more amiable terms of subjugation. They wanted to be free of a colonial empire whose entire structure, at that time, revolved around the subjugation of colonies.

Those same tensions exist between industrial food and local food.

Local food is a reaction, not against the outcomes of industrial food, but against the nature of industrial food as a system. It is not the next progression of our industrial food system like health food and organic food had been. Local food is as dramatic of a shift today as industrial food had been in the 1940's.

In other words, local food threatens industrial food. For that reason, local food will not reform industrial food.

Unlike health food and organic food, which promised to fix the ails of industrial food from within its ranks, local food offers to replace industrial food. It's a declaration of independence from a monarchical food system. Every time that another farmer takes one more acre of a grain field out of production and converts it into a vegetable garden for his local market, it's a minor rebellion. It's a decision to no longer pledge fealty to the USDA's global trade war. And it will result in—indeed, it has already resulted in—a whole new way to farm, to produce food, to buy food, and to eat.

Yet, the monarch still exists. This allegory of the American Revolution and the local food movement serves us well when we consider that today, America and Great Britain share a strong alliance and diplomatic relations. America today is a co-citizen of the world with its former subjugator. But America's independence forever changed the British Empire.

Can local food and industrial food co-exist? Likely so. But local food will fundamentally transform America's menu. We won't cease to produce grains as a nation. We likely will not cease to export them, either. But the future of farming must include a diversity of markets that give freedom back to the landowners to choose what products their farm will grow, and which markets they will serve.

In a time when our food choices have become monolithic, local food promises something that has not been said since the greatest generation returned from war in the 1940's: Our children will not shop, dine, and cook the same way that our parents did. That was true of the baby boomer generation, and it is true again today.

How will they eat, you ask? That is the central question: What is local food? In the three chapters to follow I will define the three dimensions of proximity that make local food truly local.

Dimension 1: Geographic Proximity

Was it produced in the same county, state, or region as me? Then it's local. Simple as that. Right?

Local food's "localness" can be measured across three dimensions of proximity. The first of these dimensions is the most obvious: the proximity to that food's location. In later chapters, we'll take a closer look other dimensions—who makes local food, for example? And why is local food sold locally? Why, for example, is a confined chicken barn down the street, regardless of how close its location may be, not a consideration when we talk about local food.

For now, though, we must acknowledge that the first and easiest rubric to evaluate local food is its proximity to one's geographic location. Consumers today are inclined to buy food that came from their area. Even supermarkets are getting in the game, when they can, listing the state of origin on any products that come from a nearby farm worth boasting about.

The question is: Why? What is it about a farm's distance from the buyer that could correlate to a marketable value in the food? And, does that value track linearly with distance? Is a tomato grown just 10 miles away twice as good as one grown 20 miles away?

Well, of course not. Yet many people still try to define local in an arbitrary number of miles. The various attempts at defining "local" in a terms of a simple mile radius—while conveniently easy to verify—often fail to evaluate the real value of local foods. Food raised just outside of the radius of, say, 100 miles might represent more of the value that local has to offer than an alternative source that happens to be 99 miles away.

Local Produce is Fresher.

The problem with picking fresh food is that it's not fresh for long. In a few days, lettuce wilts. Tomatoes go soft. Broccoli starts to turn yellow. The simple sugars that make snap peas and sweet corn so refreshingly sweet will turn into bland starch in a matter of days.

The farms and other players in the industrial food system are not ignorant of this problem, of course. They're quite ingenious in their solutions to it. They came up with some rather sophisticated ways of keeping food fresh. There's refrigeration, for one. Also, vacuum seals and various other manipulations in the environment of the food can delay the visible detriments of spoilage for days and weeks.

But that's not the most effective way that industrial food has found to overcome the freshness issue. If fresh foods won't stay fresh for long, then the answer seemed so elegantly simple: Don't pick fresh food.

Many consumers would be surprised to learn that the food they find ripe at the store was not picked ripe in the field. Nowhere is this approach more common than in the tomato industry. Author and journalist Barry Estabrook explained the process in detail to NPR's Ira Flatow. "Bright green tomatoes go into warehouse-like buildings," Estabrook explains. Then, "the doors are closed, and the processors turn on ethylene gas."[14]

Ethylene is a natural— "organic," even—gas that is emitted by many varieties of fruit plants during their ordinary course of ripening in nature. But when producing perishable fruits like tomatoes in an industrial system, farms can't afford to let their crop ripen in the due course of nature. If they did, the crop would never make it to the supermarket in time to be enjoyed.

Instead, the fruits are harvested prematurely. By doing so, the industry transforms transit time from being a race against nature to being the final step in the product's preparation. It's a rather industrious solution, that's for sure. But it comes at the cost of one important quality: flavor.

Tomatoes allowed to ripen on the vine will bear a markedly different, more intense flavor than those that are picked prior to maturity. Tomatoes don't just turn red as they ripen under the sun. They produce fructose, tannins, and other nutrients in those final days, too. That is, if they're allowed to ripen on the vine. Using ethylene, heat, or just the plain time they take to reach their point-of-sale will make a red tomato that appears ripe but doesn't exactly taste ripe.

So, what? Some could argue that it's better to give the American consumer limitless access to year-round fresh fruits and vegetables, even if the flavor isn't perfect. A matter of mere taste might seem easy to overlook. That is, of course, until you realize that it's not just flavor that degrades, but real nutrition as well. Important water-soluble vitamins like Vitamin C can degrade rapidly after harvest. Even under refrigeration, 15 percent of the Vitamin C in green beans will decay in seven days. In peas, it's 70 percent that's gone just one week after harvest.[15] Often times, the product hasn't even hit grocery store shelves before half or more of its essential vitamins have disintegrated.

Local food, of course, is harvested when it's prime for eating—ripe and ready to enjoy. Farmers can do so because the crop will be in a customer hands within days, if not hours. In fact, with precise management and a farmer who is keen to his or her market, it's not uncommon for produce to be picked the same day a customer takes it home.

So, if I buy local food, I can enjoy more flavorful food. I'll likely have more nutritious food. But I might just have more fragile food, too.

Survival of the Fittest

Imagine that you had to choose just one variety of tomato to eat for the rest of your life. How would you choose? You would certainly taste-test them. Texture is important, too. Nobody likes a leathery skin. If you had the means, a lab report that showed the nutritional values might even be helpful.

You probably would never ask yourself, "Which one of these tomatoes could I juggle like a circus clown without bruising the skin?"

That's because you're choosing a tomato for you to eat. But if you had to choose just one variety of tomato to feed the world, you would have to put at the top of your scorecard: How well does this variety survive a cross-country trip in the back of a semi-trailer? Based on that single criterion alone, supermarkets have curated the vast majority of their fresh food offerings in recent decades.

Most of American consumers today, now two generations removed from the rise of industrial agriculture, have no idea that a tomato could be anything other than a small red orb. Show them a purple and brown striped tomato, and they might think they've seen a carnival attraction. But in fact, they would simply be observing a food that would have been quite familiar to their grandparents at one time. But those purple and brown tomatoes--Cherokee Purple tomatoes, as they're called—are fragile. And the plants don't yield quite as much as some red tomatoes.

Also, much to the chagrin of the industrial farmer, every blossom yields fruit at different times throughout the season—a trait known as an indeterminate harvest. Being an indeterminate variety makes it impossible to harvest large amounts of the fruit with mechanized automation.

Some industrial farms still do pick tomatoes by hand, but even for that manual operation, heirloom varieties are once again troublesome. Heirloom tomatoes, such as the Cherokee Purple variety, are brilliantly colored when ripe. But the "shoulders" of the tomato—that top portion just around where the vine connects to the fruit—will remain green even after the fruit itself has ripened. This makes it difficult for field workers to visually identify, from their top-down vantage point, which fruits are ripe and ready to pick. Getting the ripe ones requires careful examination of each fruit.

For the last fifty years, in addition to seeking determinate varieties of tomatoes, growers also began to selectively breed for the trait of a fully red fruit, top-to-bottom. This meant that workers could more easily identify red tomatoes while peering down upon the plant.

In America today, we eat a selection of tomatoes that are determinate varieties of a uniform, red color. Cherokee Purple tomatoes were not the fittest tomato in the world of industrial food. It shares the same fate of Brandywines, Black Krim, and Tiger Striped tomatoes, to name a few others.

Similarly, our cuisine features just a handful of lettuce varieties with long shelf lives. Only those apple varieties that won't turn brown after being sliced are worth planting anymore. Many Americans are sadly unaware that a strawberry can be found that is ripe, juicy, and sweet throughout its entire red flesh, not just white and bland in the center. And we can't fathom a dozen of anything other than bleach-white eggs laid by a single breed of hen—the Leghorn.

If survival of the fittest is natural selection, there is nothing natural about the monolithic food choices that industrial food offers. Our supermarkets today are teeming with selections of those foods that proved fittest for industrial production, shipping, storage, or all three. They are chosen for characteristics that are fittest for the industrial food system, not for nature, nor for human health.

Local food offers a renewed ability for consumers to experience and enjoy a wide range of foods. Those Cherokee Purple tomatoes are delicious. They're dense, juicy and flavorful. The darker pigment is a visual cue to its higher levels of antioxidants. They're particularly tasty when they've ripened on the vine, too.

It's green shoulders, which created an inconvenience to hurried harvesters, are green because they contain chloroplasts—the part of a plant that absorbs sunlight and synthesizes sugar. When farmers bred for a red tomato from the stem down, they unwittingly bred for a more bitter tomato at the same time.

The challenge, of course, is that attaining those traits that are desirable for eating requires processes that run counter to industrial food. Don't expect to find a Cherokee Purple tomato— or any such heirloom variety of fruit or vegetable—at a typical supermarket. The only way to enjoy foods like this today are to buy them locally.

The Local Economy

There are some questions for which everyone knows the answer, but nobody wants to ask aloud. A few years ago, I was invited to be a panelist at an annual meeting for a farm co-op in rural Indiana. I decided to ask one of those questions to the audience.

"By a show of hands, how many of you learned to farm from your parents?" That was an easy one. Every hand went up.

"Now, keep your hands up if your son or daughter is learning to farm from you." Nearly every hand went down. It was a sobering statistic. It's a reality that farmers are well aware of, even if they don't care to be reminded of it.

The average age of a farmer today is 58.3 years[16]. Fewer and fewer people are adopting the profession. I am a part of this trend myself.

And, it's not as though what's lost in manpower is being made up for in automation or yield gains. Between 1998 and 2012, production of feed grains in the US increased a modest 2.2 percent according to the USDA. That's not bad considering the USDA also reported that we lost more than 100,000 farmers in that time.

But, if we are still holding to Earl Butz' mission to feed the world, America has to pick up the pace. During this same period, the world population grew over 18 percent.

How can there be so many new mouths to feed while our crop production remains virtually flat and the profession itself is not attracting a new generation?

The answer is simple: Industrial farming doesn't pay.

While most of America's attention has been on the economic woes around manufacturing job loss, it may surprise you to learn that Supplemental Nutrition Assistance Program ("SNAP" formerly known as "food stamps") benefits are applied at the greatest concentrations in the rural farming communities, not urban ones where factory jobs have been noticeably declining. Rural poverty is on the rise, even surpassing that of the oft-mentioned blighted urban centers. The plight of our corn belt is, in many ways, much graver than the plight of the rust belt.

According to the USDA's Economic Research Service, nearly half of all farms in America earned less than $10,000 in income in 2017. The majority of farmers, as a result, rely on off-farm income. When you consider all of this together, that means many of the factory workers facing the realities of layoffs and plant closures had only taken those factory jobs because their first job—their farms—have been less and less able to produce an income in the modern industrial food system.

The testimony of one Indiana farmer, Adam Moody, illustrates the current dynamic of farm income vividly in his interview with Agriculture.com editor Gil Gullickson:

> "While other farms had gotten larger or put animals under confinement, my dad and I had just maintained our farm size. We struggled to get by on two incomes on just a little over 300 acres. It came to a head in the spring of 1996, when hogs were nine cents a pound. My wife, Lucy, and I went to the grocery store one night, and we couldn't afford a ham. So, I went to the car in the parking lot and sat. It made no sense. I had just sold hogs for nine cents a pound, but I couldn't afford a ham in the store. It dawned on me that I wasn't raising food; I was raising commodities." [17]

A major factor in this inequity is the way food aggregation and distribution has industrialized. In the interest of efficiency, farms are larger, but they receive lower and lower prices for their goods. Revenues can only be buoyed by increasing output. Remember, "Get big or get out." Adam and Lucy had to get out, it would seem.

Today, less than 20 percent of a dollar spent at a typical supermarket will ever be seen by the farmer that grew the food.

Researchers at Iowa State University's Leopold Center for Sustainable Agriculture decided to take a closer look at whether this "getting big" and "getting out" was the best approach for farmers. The researchers focused on a 6-state region that included places hard-hit by manufacturing job loss—Detroit, Cleveland, Milwaukee, and St. Louis. Considering just a few dozen varieties of fruits and vegetables that are amenable to those Midwestern soils and climate, the study found that over $3 billion in revenue could be added to farms like Adam and Lucy's.

More than that, such a shift would have a significant impact on employment in the region, too. The study showed that shifting $3 billion of Midwestern food-dollars toward local farms, instead of imported foods, would equate to more than 12,000 new jobs—not only on the farms themselves, but also in the enterprises that support farms and food production.[18]

Local food not only has the propensity to reverse a decades-long trend in farm income decline, it can also create much farther-reaching economic impact.

The first and easiest-to-measure dimension of local food is its proximity to one's location. Food that is grown geographically local to you combats the degradation of freshness and flavor that industrial food suffers. More than that, local food also combats the degradation of your local economy, its vibrancy, and even its social fabric that industrial food has wrought for more than half a century.

Dimension 2: Relational Proximity

Measuring a local food's "localness" begins, quite obviously, with an understanding of where the food hails from on the planet. But measuring that dimension alone doesn't tell you if the food you're about to eat is everything that local food could offer. After all, it is entirely possible that industrial food could come from your own neighborhood.

Imagine living next door to a confined pork farm. Outside your kitchen window, thousands of hogs teem under one sprawling barn roof. On hot summer days, the odor is stifling. In a flash flood, its manure lagoons overflow their banks, pouring raw animal refuse into the picturesque creek that flows through your back yard. Heavy traffic of semi-trailers haul livestock on your quiet roads every week, carving ruts on curves and adding premature wear to the asphalt.

When a day comes that you might host a hog-roast for friends and family, are you knocking on that farmer's front door to buy an animal? Would you sort a single hog out of the noxious barn and bring it to a nearby butcher? Would you gleefully brag over beers in your back yard, "You know, this pork came from that barn right there?"

Likely not. For proponents of local food, certainly not.

My home state, Indiana, is home to an aptly named pork brand, Indiana Kitchens. It's just one of many American subsidiaries to a Japanese-owned meat conglomerate. The company harvests those confinement hogs by the tens of thousands at a factory in a small, northern Indiana town. Most of the pork from that factory enters the food supply as non-descript food on its way to supermarkets and restaurants all over America, and some even exported to major pork consuming nations like China.

But a small portion of the pork processed there is packaged as bacon, hams, and other cured meats under the feel-good label of "Indiana Kitchens." The label was created for distribution to supermarkets inside the state. In an effort to appeal to the growing trend of local food, the industrial food giant adopted a local food brand. After all, if it's raised [mostly] in Indiana, and harvested here in the state, so shouldn't this pork garner a marketing advantage for those qualities alone?

To the discerning consumer, Indiana Kitchens most certainly does not make local food. When a distributor tried to offer Indiana Kitchens hams nearing the Christmas season in an Indianapolis-area farmers market, their offering lasted less than one day. Amid a barrage of customer complaints, and even the threat of withdrawal by other market vendors, the product was banned by the market masters before a single ham could be sold.

Local food patrons know who makes local food. And they know Indiana Kitchens does not. But, given the company's address is clearly within the state's borders, how did anyone come to that conclusion—and, so emphatically, no less? Even the pork comes from Indiana farms, and the pork is processed at an Indiana facility, it's not considered to be local food.

This phenomenon extends to foods outside the controversial realms of confined animal operations. Even foods produced without overtly offensive practices might still fall short of being truly local food to their nearby consumers.

Indiana is also home to one of America's largest producers of tomato products, Red Gold. The company processes at least 95 percent of Indiana's entire tomato crop, and 80 percent of all Midwestern tomatoes. [19] That means if an Indiana resident lives near a tomato field, the odds are 20:1 that it's a Red Gold field.

Is a can of Red Gold tomatoes welcomed at the local farmers market? Of course not. Why? Because in any Indiana town, the odds may be 20:1 that a tomato field is grown for Red Gold, but the odds are only 1 in 500 that the tomatoes being sold at that farmers market came from a nearby field. Although Red Gold is a local company to Indiana, there are no means for its Indiana patrons to know the farmer who grew the food in any given can, much less build community with that farmer, and ultimately build trust with that farmer.

Measuring one's proximity to the food's location is an empirical measurement. I can count the miles, feet, and inches between my table and the farmer's field. But measuring one's proximity to the farmer themselves—to know more than where, but also who my food came from—is a relational measurement. It's measured in emotional and cognitive connection, not geographic.

Calling the 1-800 number on the back of a steel can to ask a question about my food connects me with someone whose knowledge of my food's actual origins is theoretical at-best. Seeing the paid actors in a Red Gold advertisement, or naming a pork product "Indiana Kitchens," is an attempt to artificially connect me to the people my purchase honors.

Local food not only connects people with the soils nearest to them, it connects people with the growers nearest to them. Local food is about more than a mile.

A proximity to the food's geographic location improves many aspects of the food's qualities—freshness, flavor, and nutrition—but a close relational proximity to the people who produce the food improves far more than food quality. It improves trust, social connection and community.

Human Food.

Early one August morning, Scott Wilson had parked his truck-and-trailer at the back door of my vegetable processing plant in Greenfield, Indiana. Scott was one of the local farmers who grew corn for us to blanch, cut, and freeze. We then distributed his corn, and other farmers' corn, to grocery stores around the Midwest. On that morning, Scott came up to the office to find me.

"Hey, you got a sec?" he said as he knocked on the office door and peeked his head in.

"Of course." I always enjoyed the interactions with our farmers.

"I'm getting direct messages from your customers asking about seed varieties and chemicals and stuff." He started. "And, I mean a lot of them."

I started to interrupt with an apology. "Sorry. Yeah. Um. They probably found you through that code we print on the bag. And…"

I was nervous that the intrusion might have been an unwanted one. In most industrial supplier-distributor relationships, the distribution company doesn't pass customer-service issues up the value chain like this. Maybe, I feared, farmers like Scott wouldn't want to get inquiries from the customers directly.

"No. No. It's great," he interrupted me. "I just didn't know what you wanted me to tell them."

What did I want him to tell them? The truth. That would have been obvious, I thought.

"There's no script. Just answer their questions." I told Scott.

"I spray, you know." He said as if he was suddenly in a confessional booth.

"I should hope so. We don't want to sell bags of worms." Due to our climate, moth larvae are prolific in non-GMO sweet corn in Indiana, especially in late summer. The only defense is sprayed pesticides.

"Ok. I can tell them that?" Scott was under the impression there might be some spin we wanted to convey—a truth to obfuscate, perhaps.

"You tell them how you grow their food, Scott. If you're proud of how you do it, and you'd feed it to your kids, you just tell them why that is."

Not only was the intrusion not an annoyance to Scott, it was a welcomed opportunity to connect with the people who delighted in Scott's food.

Over time, the messages weren't purely interrogations, either. Scott received gratitude. Customers shared memories of how their grandparents used to freeze corn the same way we did for Scott. Scott's corn, frozen in a bag that identified Scott as the grower, reminded them of home, of family, and of a kind of food they had all but forgotten.

For Scott, the messages reminded him of why he chose to farm the way that he farmed.

For our customers, the ability to reach the actual producer of the food rekindled a long-lost human component to food that people—both customers and farmers—seemed to miss. In an agricultural industry that dehumanizes its producers, and in turn its customers as well, knowing who grew your food is more than just emotionally satisfying. It serves a functional purpose in the food supply chain as well.

Just as I had told Scott, for farmers these interactions are about standing behind their work. If the farmer would feed his family these goods, then tell the customer that. The converse is also true: if there's something unsafe or risky in the food, this process provides an accountability to food quality that no set of rules or regulations could ever replace.

In Scott's case, he wasn't asked to write an impersonal advertising blurb about his product to be used in marketing. He was answering an individual. He was responding to individuals who were empowered to know Scott's identity, and who had empowered Scott to know theirs.

Regulations are not bad. But they serve the food industry only where human connection cannot.

For example, take Scott's confession "I spray." Those sprays that Scott uses are safe, provided that the clearing times are strictly followed. Clearing times are the prescribed amount of time that must pass between the last spray and the harvest. If Scott harvested before the clearing time had elapsed, he wouldn't let his family touch that food. And he wouldn't let your family touch it, either.

The same kind of litmus can't be assumed with an industrial farmer, because they grow for contracts that usually prevent them from even being permitted to eat their own crop. Everything must be committed to the contract holder—an aggregating company such as Red Gold, for example. If weather prevented the farmer from spraying when he had planned, he may face price penalties for missing a harvest deadline. The clearing time has not been met, but there is little more than a few lines in a contract that prevent the farmer from harvesting anyway. The social constructs that impose upon Scott to harvest safe food aren't brought to bear on these industrial growers.

For Scott, he knows the names and the faces of people in his community that might experience adverse reactions—a rash around the mouth, perhaps flu-like symptoms for a short time, or in the most extreme cases, developmental issues, birth defect, and increased cancer risks. For these reasons, no farmer would take the same crop from that questionable harvest and feed it to his own family. But it's far too easy to justify rule-bending in one's own mind when the human impact of those bent rules is imperceptible.

A wage-earning worker can shirk procedures that lead to a foodborne illness—an all too familiar scenario in today's food industry—and doing so certainly lacks integrity. But for a farmer to knowingly offer contaminated food to a mother with kids in tow at their local farmers market—to look her in the eye, smile, and thank her for making a purchase that puts her family in peril—lacks more than just integrity. It lacks humanity.

Had industrial food merely failed the American consumer in areas of freshness and flavor, then the industry would have solved those problems alone with industrial solutions. Indeed, many advances have already been made in industrial food to bring certain qualities of industrial food closer in line with that of geographically local food. But industrial food failed the American consumer in ways far beyond the physical properties of the food itself. Industrial food lacks trust and community—things that no improvement to industrial process could ever restore.

It feels like farming again.

When I first visited Indy Family Farms, I was skeptical that they could ever be a local food vendor. We were always looking for more suppliers in the area, and this farm contacted us to inquire about processing their strawberries. I decided to pay a visit.

Pulling off the highway onto their gravel drive, I could see immediately that this was not the kind of farm I envisioned. I drove toward a large, newly constructed barn. Parked outside was a 24-row John Deere planter—a mainstay of large, industrial grain farms. Through the barn's open doors, I could see the four-wheel-drive tractor that must have pulled the planter that spring. A collection of other implements was in view—sprayers, grain wagons, even a semi-truck and trailer.

This was an industrial farm. What was I doing here?

But as I walked to the office in the corner of the barn, I could see a small field where strawberry plants were growing. That was the subject of our meeting that day.

Cathy is a sharp woman, I soon learned. She and her husband farmed many thousands of acres of grain southwest of Indianapolis, and they did quite well at it.

But we weren't there to discuss any of that. Cathy wanted her strawberries—just three acres, mind you—to be in local markets. And despite her mastery of the global grain trade, selling food to her local community was something new for her. That's why I was there.

After some time discussing pricing, possible outlets, and what kind of revenues she could expect in her first year, I mustered the courage to ask: "If I may, what made you decide to raise strawberries? It's a far cry from corn and soybeans."

Cathy looked out her window for a moment and thought. Her gaze seemed to look right past that industrial planter parked outside. Then she answered. "That just didn't feel like farming anymore."

I had no reply. I knew exactly what she meant. I just nodded in agreement.

Do not overlook the fact that farmers in the industrial food system are the ones most impacted, not the shoppers. Which means that protests, demonstrations and attacks on any given farm or farmer is misguided. The Arkansas farmer with barns full of confined chicken and the Iowa farmer with thousands of acres of monoculture corn are no more at fault for the state of industrial food than a taxi driver is responsible for traffic jams. They're each fulfilling a task that they've been given in a greater system that was poorly designed. While both would love a way out, as farmers like Cathy could tell you, converting to local food production is a high-risk, terrifying venture.

But it's a venture that everyone, both consumers and farmers alike, are seeking more and more. For the consumer, knowing who grew your food makes it local. For farmers, knowing who ate your food feels like farming again.

Dimension 3: Natural Proximity

We have seen that local food is, quite obviously, found in close physical proximity—and there are benefits of that proximity. We have seen, also, that local food is a matter of relational proximity— how close am I to the person or people who produced this food?

But how does local food intersect with natural food—that quality that many have looked to the USDA's Organic label to signify? Is there a way of measuring a food's nearness to nature, and, if so, to what extent should labels and certifications play a role? After all, if the earliest detected problems with industrial food were its harsh chemical usage and artificiality, then how does a food's proximity do anything to resolve those foundational problems?

Why would local food be considered the definitive reaction against industrial food? To answer that question, we must understand what industrial food promised. Indeed, industrial food succeeded in doing just what it was designed to do. What was that design? And, just how much did we need it to begin with?

A Solution in Search of a Problem.

Years ago, in preparation for a tradeshow, I purchased a refurbished tablet to have at the booth. I anticipated a large number of visitors during short bursts of time in between sessions, so I wanted to have a solution that would make it fast and easy for me to quickly demo our product—a software—on the floor of the exposition hall to passers-by.

It worked. For two days, that small investment enabled me to collect dozens of interested leads. It paid for itself many times over. I am glad that I made the purchase.

But when the show was over, it had a new role in my office: paperweight.

We don't attend tradeshows often at all. In the months that followed, I was haunted by this rather expensive purchase I had made that was no longer in any meaningful use. So, I set out to find a new use for the tablet.

At first, I loaded presentations onto it and led meetings from the tablet instead of my laptop. But its presentation capabilities were limited, and I soon reverted to using my laptop for presentations. Meanwhile, our operations manager was using an old-fashioned clipboard, pen, and paper to log errors in the shop. I devised what I thought would be an ingenious new digital entry system that employed the tablet. As it turned out, though, it was faster and more efficient to jot down information in real time and enter the data later at a computer than to be troubled by the tablet's interface while trying to get a job done.

The tablet had been a solution to a finite problem, and it worked. It met a very real need, and aptly so. But after the tradeshow ended, that problem ceased to exist. My efforts to re-deploy it were costing me more time and energy than just retiring the device and moving on.

This phenomenon is known as "a solution in search of a problem." People fall victim to this kind of thinking all the time. Everyone has a stash of old clothes that no longer fit, but we just can't bear to dispose of them. How many toolsheds are filled with once-useful appliances that just need a little repair, as soon as we get around to it?

Such was the state of the American military industrial complex as of Victory Day in Europe, 1945.

When the G.I.'s first set sail for the European theater in the early 1940's, America was not in need of cheese-like powder that could never spoil. American consumers were not desperate to find a just-add-water dinner option. We didn't even pine for out-of-season fruits in the Northern states, nor were meat producers stifled by the inability to transport their product thousands of miles safely—after all, there were plenty of mouths to feed just miles from the local butcher.

The industrious people who made feeding our troops across the globe possible deserve much credit. Their innovations played no small part in the Allied victory. But when the last trenches were filled in, and the last Pacific outpost was abandoned, their inventions became like that tablet in my office. The thought of having such a technological power at our fingertips and not deploying simply couldn't be fathomed.

Seemingly overnight, supermarkets sprang up in place of local grocers. National brands of powdered-this and canned-that dominated not only store shelves but also the weeknight menus in homes across America.

Bananas and grapes became year-round staples in every household. Fresh lettuce salad could be served anytime, anywhere. Inexpensive lands in Arkansas were put to use producing massive amounts of chicken for the entire nation to enjoy at a savings. Dust-lands in Kansas were stacked tail-deep with cattle. Barns were erected all over the Midwest to house pigs by the millions.

A solution in search of a problem promised to bring the American food consumer the same thing that it brought to the American troops: transportable food, and imperishable food.

Therein lies an important clue to why America today is increasingly turning toward local food. It's not entirely that local food is a unique solution itself. It's that industrial food solves problems that Americans are realizing they don't face, and at costs that we no longer want to bear.

In some respects, local food isn't an alternative. It's the norm. The alternative—industrial food—has been a national experiment for over half a century, and it's causing more problems than it solves.

Input. Output. Waste.

Industrialization is a good thing, to be sure. No natural process exists that could create automobiles—enter Henry Ford's assembly line. No natural process will arrange words on a page like you find in this book—enter the Heidelberg press. There is not even a natural process that combines elements into an alloy with the strength of steel—enter Carnegie's steel mills.

The same, however, cannot be said of food. Industrialization allowed us to create more food, faster, and with less human effort. It's true. But unlike the aforementioned industries, the industrialization of food has proven far less efficient than nature at producing the food we need, when we need it.

Industrial processes work on a simple formula of input, output, and waste. Inputs such as iron ore, minerals, and fuel for heat are used to create the output of steel. But in the process, wastes such as ash, smoke, and slag are also created.

Natural processes, on the other hand, produce no waste. Ecosystems exist on the notion of a closed loop. One organism's waste becomes another's input, and so on.

Beef and poultry farming are two of the clearest examples of nature's unmatched efficiency in food production. Cattle do not have stomachs, per se. Instead, they have rumens—a four-stage organ where cellulose like grass is broken down through fermentation until it becomes usable energy. That grass, however, thrives on soil rich in carbon, phosphorous, potassium, and nitrogen. Not surprisingly, three of these four elements are prevalent in the cow's manure.

Cows eat grass. Grass eats manure. And on and on it goes, except for one little twist. Peer out over a pasture that's exclusively grazed by cattle and you will be sure to see dense, large clumps of tall grass that the cattle seem to reject as they forage for food. Why? Because that grass is growing right up from a clump of their own manure—a "cow pie" as they're called—and cattle, like any animal, are smart enough not to eat their own waste.

Smart farmers, however, are masters of managing nature—learning from it, mimicking it—and not combatting it. What farmers had noted on the American plains was that nature's poultry—pheasant and quail—seemed to migrate in a pattern that followed bison. A few days after bison had grazed a pasture, you could be sure to find fowl there.

What were those fowl doing there? Looking for larvae, of course. Insects are quick to lay their eggs in the warm piles of manure. After a few days, those eggs are hatched, and the fowl go hunting. Their hunt requires scraping the manure piles apart. Observe any bird standing on the ground and you'll notice that they habitually scrape at the ground with their claws in search of insects and larvae.

The net result is the spreading of manure in such a way that would allow those same bison to return and graze indiscriminately a few weeks later.

Farmers who seek to maximize nature's productivity—not replace it with industrial processes—took note of this trend over a century ago. Cattle and poultry go hand-in-hand in a natural farming system.

There was one more aspect of this natural symbiosis that has been observed by farmers for centuries but, interestingly, the industrial era helped to finally explain. My grandfather knew that if a pasture seemed anemic, he needed to run chickens over it. It was the kind of conventional wisdom that passed on from generation to generation of farmers, even if none of them could articulate the chemistry behind it.

It wasn't until the chemical era of farming that we came to know grass thrives on carbon, phosphorous, potassium, and nitrogen. While cow manure is rich in three of these four, it lacks a significant source of nitrogen. And what animal produces large amounts of nitrogen in its manure? Poultry, of course.

One must wonder, then, if such an obvious and simple natural process exists for producing beef and poultry, why would any industrial process be proposed, much less adopted? Because the solution found its problem—or so it seemed.

While a cow's rumen is best suited for fermenting grass, if fed grain the animal would fatten faster. Compressing time-to-market from 24 months on grass to just 18 months on corn translates to a 16 percent increase in productivity. What's more, the land requirements for feeding grass can range from two to six acres per animal. If feeding only corn, conceivably the animal need only have enough space to turn around in. Today, farmers measure their land's capacity in cattle per acre, not acres per cow. Of course, the chickens could be packed even more densely—stacking cages vertically on the same square footage.

For decades, the seeming brilliance of this industrialization was lauded by farmers, agronomists, and even the consumer. Corn-fed beef became a buzz word at meat counters and butcher shops in the 1970s and '80s.

It was a problem with soil erosion that first exposed the flaws in this system. Top soil from the Midwest was being found in the Mississippi river delta by the millions of tons. Without the return of that cow's manure to the soil where its food had been grown, unseen values like subterranean fungal networks, microbial growth, and natural permaculture all but disappeared. As a result, topsoil is rinsed away with every rain that falls on barren dirt.

The output manure of the beef production is no longer being utilized as an input for the corn production—an oversight that nature never makes.

The same was true for chicken manure's nitrogen. In lieu of poultry droppings, farmers turned to an industrial byproduct of natural gas production—anhydrous ammonia—to deposit nitrogen into their anemic soils. Forget the conventional wisdom of grandpa—we now had a more progressive approach. But while chicken manure had always been free and plentiful, natural gas is a non-renewable resource. The cost of natural gas production is on the rise, which means that precious nitrogen fertilizer cost is rising as well. The cost to a farmer for that anhydrous ammonia has increased over 400 percent since 1980.[20]

Farmers now pay dearly for inputs like nitrogen, which had once been self-promulgating from the hens they kept in a natural farming system.

When the natural cycle is broken, those inputs and outputs leave something that is totally foreign to nature: waste. The various industrial solutions to this problem are mounting in cost. Water pollution, soil erosion, and most notable to the consumer are the outbreaks of E. coli—a bacteria proliferated in a cow's rumen when that animal is fed too much grain.

Farming to the Test.

One of the criticisms of standardized testing in education has been the tendency to "teach to the test." The problem is quite simple to understand: First, we come up with a measurable way to determine whether someone has mastered a subject. That's the test. But once the test exists, learning molds to the test, as if the ultimate goal is passing the test, not mastery of the subject. In the most extreme circumstances, students are taught methods and memorizations that allow them to pass the test without ever truly understanding the subject.

The same has happened in local food. Organic farming was one of the earliest examples. Once the food industry determined that there was marketable value in deeming some foods as "organic," the USDA stepped in to design a measurable way to determine if a farmer had mastered the subject. Certification was akin to a test, and farmers began to "farm to the test," in a manner of speaking. Before long, even industrial farmers had figured out how to pass the test while never even acknowledging the values that shaped organic farming from its genesis.

We see this kind of test mastery—or perhaps even test tampering—taking place in all categories of food. It's become popular to produce brown eggs, passing a visual test for some semblance of quality or differentiation, while never actually adapting the farming practices to master the kind of farming that made brown eggs synonymous with quality eggs in the first place. The produce section at many supermarkets is beginning to diversify their offerings of tomatoes with varying colors and shapes of tomatoes, reminiscent of the farmers market selection, yet still producing those crops with the same industrial methods as before.

Perhaps the most prominent example of farming to the test is in the proliferation of the "grass-fed" label on beef. Grass-fed beef gained popularity among discerning consumers, not because the grass diet itself was the single test of quality beef, but because it was one mark of a farming method that—as discussed earlier in this chapter—reduces waste by mimicking the natural process.

Feeding grass became the test. Feeding grain, for some purists, became a failure. And, as expected, farmers began farming to the test.

The test is easier to pass for farmers in warmer climates, such as Australia, New Zealand, and Brazil where grass grows year-round. The symbiosis of poultry in the rotational grazing process is completely overlooked, however.[21] That question never appears on the grass-fed test, so why learn the material?

Adam Moody, founder of Moody's Butcher Shops, tells the sad account of one farmer whose fear of failing the grass-fed test had disastrous consequences for his animals. After receiving a load of underweight, pneumonia-stricken cattle at the slaughter facility one particularly cold Indiana February, Adam advised the farmer that he needed to increase his herd's calorie intake. But the farmer insisted that he was striving for 100 percent grass-fed animals and would feed only hay despite the bitter cold.

The farmer missed the point of grass-fed beef altogether. When a scoop of barley, or even corn, could mean the difference between an animal having the energy to maintain body fat for insulation and energy levels to fight infection, then the test is wrong. Mastery of the grass-fed subject is not about the cow's diet alone. No farming method can be reduced to a formula. But the farmer feared negative reactions from would-be consumers if they learned that he fed grain to his cattle.

Therein lies the problem. It's hard not to farm to the test when the consumers are often the ones grading the exam, and most consumers don't have their Ph.D. in farming.

What America needs from local food is not a perfect score on a true-false exam: grass-fed, no cages, pesticide-free, no additives, and so on. We need food that's valued as a community, not commodities. As consumers, we must learn to scrutinize that food through the lens of relationship, not rhetoric.

Finding Local Food.

When the certified organic program first arose, the appeal for consumers was strong. Amid a cloud of uncertainty regarding food's health and safety, that small circle imprinted on a label promised to put all fear to rest. Whereas reports of chemicals, pesticides, and fertilizers cast a pall on any food-buying decision, one simple claim seemed to put all right again. The prospect of being able to discern good food with just a glance at the label eventually proved too good to be true. Organic food, after all, is still produced industrially.

Unlike organic food, however, finding local food is difficult. Not only because the market for local food is less convenient than the corner store or the supermarket just off the highway, but because of the seemingly complex amount of due diligence required to verify a food's source—due diligence that little round "organic" label purported to do for you. How can a layperson, unfamiliar with the inner workings of chicken manure, cattle rumens, tomato chloroplasts, and the decay rates of water-soluble vitamins possibly choose good food for his or her family? And, after visiting a farmers market for the first time, many ask themselves if they can afford local food once they find it.

Local food, as a reaction against industrial food, will never take center stage in the grocery industry—in the way that health food and organic food have—until finding local food is something that everyone knows how to do.

Three Dimensions of Local Food

In the previous three chapters, you learned what local food really is. There are three dimensions by which we measure local food. It's not merely, as the name could imply, food from a geographically nearby source. The three dimensions of local food are as follows:

1. **Geographic Proximity**.
    Your distance to the physical location where the food was produced is the first of three ways to measure a food's localness.
2. **Relational Proximity**.
    Your distance, relationally speaking, to a real person(s) responsible for producing the food is another way to measure a food's localness.
3. **Natural Proximity**.
    How nearly the food's production resembles natural processes is the third, and perhaps most difficult to measure, dimension of a food's localness.

This three-step approach, while not quite as convenient as the organic certification insignia, provides a simple and understandable rubric for examining local food. It has an almost immediate familiarity in that it captures succinctly a set of ideals that local food advocates have struggled to canonize.

The shorthand is flexible, too. People have referred to this as "3D" local food. Using that terminology, we can also conveniently categorize and define some foods that, while they aren't fully local, still appeal to a similar set of values that local food entails. We can admit, for example that some foods are at least two-thirds local. I may have a relationship to a food artisan that produces clean-label snack food using ingredients from sources they know and trust, too. But they produce the food a thousand miles away. I have proximity in the relationship. The food has proximity to nature. But there is no proximity to the location. It's two-thirds local, and that doesn't necessarily disqualify it from my menu.

Relationships are the Key.

If you had to pick one new habit to focus on—one new thing to shop for when buying food—I think that America has focused on the wrong metric for too long. We've developed rubrics for geographic proximity: food miles, country of origin laws (COOL), source identification, etc. And shoppers have been trained to weigh their food on the balance of miles alone.

That's not bad, per se. But it does create a sort of "farming to the test" paradigm that becomes all to easy of a box to check.

If, instead, we begin to focus more on the relational proximity that we have to our food, then both the geographic and the natural proximities will come into line more naturally. Relationship is the one dimension that has a natural affect on the other two.

Focusing on food miles alone, we could eat unnatural food from a farmer we could never know (e.g. the CAFO next door). Focusing on the natural qualities alone, we end up with "certified" organic products imported from other nations.

But if the one thing—the key quality—that we insisted on finding in our food wasn't a distance or a certification, but rather a connection to the food producer, then that force alone actually impacts the other two dimensions. It's more likely that I will find a connection to the grower when that grower is nearby. And, it's more likely that the grower will be using honorable practices when they know their farm, even their own name, is visible to the end-consumer.

I'm not suggesting that you ignore the other two dimensions. On the contrary, the only way to address them is to consider the relational dimension first. If you seek to ask about the food's origin or how it was grown, the first thing you'll actually discover is whether anyone with an answer is within your reach. If they aren't, then you're not buying local food. And if they are, the odds are high that they geographically close, or using natural processes, or both.

Measuring Nature.

Putting a measurement on the first dimension—proximity to the location—is easy. Even the second dimension, although it's less concrete than the first, is a distance that's easy to sense. Start asking questions about the food, and you will quickly learn whether you have a relationship with someone who is involved in the food's production or not. And, more importantly, whether you can be placed in contact with such a person.

It's the third dimension that can be intimidating to measure. For instance, when I suggest that you start asking questions about the food, you might be wondering: What questions?

Without a degree in biology, how can the average consumer be expected to assess the validity of a farm or food artisan's practices?

The reality is much simpler than it sounds. First, understand what separates a natural process from an industrial one: input, output, and waste. Then, ask about the differential.

Industrial processes defy nature. The forces of nature have to be mitigated, not mimicked, in industrial food. One simple question that any layperson can ask of a farmer or food artisan is this:

> *Where could I find food being produced like this in nature?*

A grass-fed farmer, even one who supplements some grain, would love to tell you about rumenid animals, perennial prairies, carbon cycles, and so on. A corn-fed beef farmer has no answer for this simple question.

Horticulturalists will love to tell of the symbiosis of basil and tomatoes, foliar feeding and beneficial fungi as a pest control measure. Industrial, monoculture vegetable farmers will have little to describe, if you can reach the farmer at all. Nobody on the other end of a 1-800 number will be able to muster these answers from their call scripts.

The second question to ask is similar to the first. Understanding that the key differential between natural processes and industrial ones is the cycle of input, output and waste, you can simply put the questions like this:

> *What kind of inputs does your process require?*
> *How do you manage the waste or byproducts?*

Producers of local food will boast of compost piles, regenerative soil health, building soils, and wasting nothing. Industrial farmers cannot farm without inputs, and they are motivated to reduce waste only when the cost to dispose of it becomes noticeable.

Even processed foods can be run through this inquisition. Food artisans who create breads, sauces, meals, and entrees with natural ingredients and processes are often quite proud of the natural preservatives they've discovered and the elegant simplicity of their recipes.

Seeking Diversity.

There is another way to seek out local food that doesn't require an inquisition of the farmer. Now that we have identified the opposite of local food—Industrial Food—one shopping approach is to simply watch out for the qualities that define it. Recall that industrial food is grown with specialization, which enables repeatable processes and scale.

By deduction, then, you can know that a farmer who raises a diverse mix of products is likely not creating industrial food.

A produce farmer that sells nothing but lettuce, for example, has adopted industrialized means to control his pests and handle his waste. More diverse growers use rotations, companion planting, and even beneficial insects to grow their crops. These methods don't scale, and they are not effective if the farm specializes in just one crop.

In fact, some vegetable farmers will also offer poultry or eggs. Why? Because the chickens are natural insect predators, first of all. But what's more, those chickens will eat vegetable scraps—

damaged or poor-quality crops—and their waste makes a nutrient-rich compost for the next season.

It's a simple and elegant approach to farming, but it doesn't scale. It doesn't scale because it's not a specialized, single-crop, farm.

The same is true for livestock growers. Rarely could a beef producer offer quality, local beef using natural processes if he or she produces just beef alone. An exclusively beef farmer smacks of industrial food, whereas local food vendors will have a diverse offering of beef, pork, and chicken. Pork and chickens both, as we discussed in a previous chapter, produce higher nitrogen content in their manures, which in-turn creates richer pastures for the beef.

There's another reason that local food producers diversify, as well. Without the government-backed subsidy plans that buffer industrial farmers against losses, local food producers have to buffer themselves against potential crop loss. Diversification is the simplest and smartest way to do so.

Even some of the most prevalent specializations, such as orchards, will have diversity at the local food scale. Any healthy orchard that wants to avoid industrial processes will have bee hives on-site, too. It's not uncommon to find local orchards offering both apples and honey under the same brand.

Above all, the most important thing to seek out in local food is not attributes of the food itself, or a checklist of farm practices, but a relationship with the producer. Many of the ways that I have listed for finding local food cannot be known without that connection, and many of these sought-after qualities of local food become obvious when such a relational connection is found.

The Cost of ~~Local~~ Food.

I used to get mad. I got really mad. When a would-be customer would tell me that buying local was "too expensive" for their budget, I would roll my eyes and offer no sympathy. It was infuriating.

Until my wife pointed something out to me: Local food is expensive, sometimes.

She would know, of course, being the one who shops for groceries in our family. And she was right. She pulled out frozen broccoli, 89 cents. Bread—and good bread, mind you—two or three dollars a loaf. Pre-sliced, no less. A container of spring mix salad, twice the size as any farmer vends at a farmers market, but not quite twice the price.

"Who cares," I objected. "A buck or less difference… who cares?"

But, for a family of five that eats like ours, those small variances on every item really add up. Add to that the fact that your local farmer doesn't run sales every week like the supermarket does, and if you're a deal shopper you can be looking at an objective difference of double or even triple your accustomed grocery budget to shop all local food.

What gives?

First of all, not all local food is the same. If you divide local *artisan* food from the comparable staples that can be sourced either locally or from non-local equivalents—and I do mean equivalents—then you'll quickly see that the price gulf is not uniform.

That means your run-of-the-mill cucumbers, lettuce, pork chops and eggs are not dramatically more expensive locally than their comparable non-local counterparts. Simple foods like these may be incrementally more expensive, but not by orders of magnitude. A dozen grass-pastured eggs can be found matching all dimensions of local food for a percentage more, sometimes the same or less, than comparable brown eggs at the supermarket having none of the local dimensions. The same is often true of your staple vegetables, and even pasture-raised meats.

Could they be incrementally more expensive? A percentage more than industrial food? Sure. But they're not double or triple the price. They're not nearly as far removed from the expected price as, say, artisan cheeses or charcuterie might be.

It's in other categories where the real sticker shock usually sets in. "Six dollars for cheese," one friend once complained to me, "I can get a bag of Kraft for 99 cents!" Or, consider a locally-crafted soup or entrée. $10 to $14 for a quart of frozen soup is commonplace at the farmers market, compared to 99-cent cans at the grocery store. A hard salami from a local chef is not to be compared with a Slim-Jim at the gas station.

Here is what you need to realize in these categories: you're paying for artisan craftsmanship, not commodity food. When it comes to locally-sourced prepared foods and value-added items, the preparation is expensive because it's manual. It's hand-crafted and a qualitatively a different item.

So, if cost is your biggest concern—or even a concern at all—you probably don't splurge much on these kinds of items, whether they're local or not. You probably buy semi-custom suits, not individually-tailored ones. You buy the $5.99 wine special instead of hunting around for a good vintage year. Your home may be stocked with name-brand furniture, but not custom-made and hand-stitched.

Buying local does not have to mean subsidizing a starving artist. There are some artisans who are not selling local food. They're selling experiences, and you might just not be in the market for that these days. There is no guilt in buying non-local bread. You know why? Because there might not be a local alternative. Just because its bread doesn't make it a true market alternative for everyday sandwich bread. Know what you're buying.

Can you really afford industrial food?

It's also worth asking yourself at times: Why is the industrial food so cheap?

When I was in the frozen corn business, we paid more to the farmer for a pound of raw corn than you would spend on a fully cut, processed, blanched, and canned pound of corn at the supermarket. Try to compete with that!

But how could this be? Were we terrible negotiators? Or, maybe we were buying from inefficient farmers with overly high costs? Neither was the case. We were paying what the corn actually costs. Our competitors weren't.

First of all, local food is not subsidized like industrial food is. So, in many subtle ways, the real cost of growing industrial food is shared among the taxpayers. That can mean cheap food prices in the aisle, but hidden costs adding up in myriad other ways you don't see at the cash register.

Second, you may have noticed that canned corn doesn't taste all that good. Nor, for that matter, do the cheap versions of frozen corn. Merely packing starch into a light-yellow waxy kernel that resembles sweetcorn does not make it sweetcorn. It just doesn't work that way. Instead, what cheap food providers are buying is, in most cases, water or air. Sometimes both.

In the case of our corn competitors. They bought poor-quality (perhaps seconds, or grade-B) corn. That often means it's grown too long in the field. When corn is over-mature, it enlarges on the stalk. But as it matures, it toughens and dehydrates slightly. As a result, it's cheaper to purchase that over-matured corn from the farmer.

Not to worry, though. Heat the corn to 260-degrees in a steam bath and it gets right back to edible. It soaks up a fair amount of moisture, too. Sure, 79 cents per pound may be a cheap price for corn, but it's a monstrous markup on water.

Something similar is happening with your fresh produce. You like the looks of those strawberries, don't you? Plump, red, and huge. Ever notice the hollow cavity on the inside after you bite into it? A pint of strawberries isn't a pint anymore. What about your bell peppers? Compare the size of a bell pepper at a supermarket to the size of one at a farmers market and you're likely to think the farmer just doesn't have what it takes to grow bigger peppers. Until, that is, you cut into them. One has a thick, dense flesh all the way around. The other is tantamount to a green balloon.

Ultimately, no matter how much I adjust the scales for things like water-weight, air volume, subsidy, and quality differentiators, replacing your entire grocery budget with local food might still be out of reach. Don't fret. Fill your pantry with 79 cent corn and 99 cent cans of soup. Eat, for goodness sake, eat!

But where you can and when you can, squeeze locally-made goods into your budget at every corner. As more farmers find more local customers for their goods, the market grows, and prices fall. It's a basic principal of economics. Which means that every dollar spent on local food today is an investment in a future that your kids will appreciate. Because if we continue to do this, the day will come when eating healthy and playing one's role in the local economy won't be the expensive choice anymore.

Many people ask: Can I afford local food? But I ask: When the costs are added up—environmental costs, relational costs, health costs—can we really afford industrial food? What America needs from local food can't be measured in miles. We need a food system that won't cost us our nation's health, our land and water, and the very relationships that weave the fabric of community.

About the Author

Nick Carter was born and raised on a small, Indiana farm near Russiaville, Indiana. After leaving the farm, he founded several technology startups in Indianapolis. In 2016, he blended his technology experience with his passion for local food, co-founding an online farmers market that delivers. His mission is to enable food producers to thrive in their local and regional markets. Nick and his wife Kendra reside on their own 20-acre farm near Indianapolis where, together with their three children, they raise food for their community.

---

[1] USDA Agricultural Marketing Service. "National Organic Program: USDA Organic Regulations." *Federal Register* 82, no. 53, (2017). 14420-14425. https://www.federalregister.gov/documents/2017/03/21/2017-05480/national-organic-program-usda-organic-regulations.

[2] USDA. "National Organic Program – International Trade Arrangements and Agreements." USDA. September 2017. Accessed November 25, 2018. https://www.usda.gov/oig/webdocs/01601-0001-21.pdf.

[3] The Hartman Group. *Organic & Natural 2014.* 2014.

[4] Norman, A. G. "Advances in Agronomy." Academic Press (1956).

[5] The Associated Press. "Farmer Suicide Rate Swells in 1980's, Study Says." NY Times. October 14, 1991. Accessed November 18, 2018. https://www.nytimes.com/1991/10/14/us/farmer-suicide-rate-swells-in-1980-s-study-says.html.

[6] "Assets, Debt, and Wealth." USDA Economic Research Service. Accessed November 20, 2018. https://www.ers.usda.gov/topics/farm-economy/farm-sector-income-finances/assets-debt-and-wealth/.

[7] "Census of Agriculture Historical Archive." USDA (2017).

[8] "Trade." USDA Economic Research Service. Accessed November 12, 2018. https://www.ers.usda.gov/topics/crops/corn-and-other-feedgrains/trade/

[9] NKJV. Matthew 5:37

[10] "The 2016 Food Revolution Study." Label Insight. Accessed November 10, 2018. https://www.labelinsight.com/foodrevolutionstudy

[11] Kelly, William. "Rodale Press and Organic Gardening." Paper presented at the History of the Organic Movement Workshop (88th ASHS Annual Meeting), The Pennsylvania State University, University Park, July 1991. Accessed November 10, 2018. https://hort.purdue.edu/newcrop/pdfs/History_Organic_Movement.pdf.

[12] "Frequently Asked Questions (FAQ)." ACGA. Accessed November 10, 2018. https://communitygarden.org/resources/faq/

[13] "Farmers' Markets." Agricultural Marketing Resource Center. Accessed November 10, 2018. https://www.agmrc.org/markets-industries/food/farmers-markets

[14] "The Unsavory Story of Industrially-Grown Tomatoes." National Public Radio. August 26, 2011. Accessed November 15, 2018. https://www.npr.org/2011/08/26/139972669/the-unsavory-story-of-industrially-grown-tomatoes.

[15] Barrett, Diane. "Maximizing the Nutritional Value of Fruits and Vegetables." *Food Technology* 61, no. 4 (2007). 40-44. http://www.fruitandvegetable.ucdavis.edu/files/197179.pdf.

[16] "The Average Age of An American Farmer." Food Dialogues. Accessed November 10, 2018. https://www.fooddialogues.com/article/average-age-american-farmer/.

[17] Gullickson, G. "Farmers For the Future: Purpose-Driven Farming." Agriculture. March 30, 2010. Accessed November 15, 2018. https://www.agriculture.com/successful-farming/family/farmers-f-future-purposedriven-farming_123-ar6269.

[18] Harvie, Alicia and Steffrey, Hilde. "Rebuilding America's Economy with Family Farm-Centered Food Systems." Farm Aid. June, 2010. Accessed November 15, 2018. https://www.farmaid.org/our-work/family-farmers/rebuilding-americas-economy-with-family-farm-centered-food-systems/.

[19] Choettle, Anhony. "Indiana's Red Gold becomes a tomato-industry big boy". *Indiana Business Journal*, August 31, 2006. Accessed November 15, 2018. https://indianaeconomicdigest.com/main.asp?SectionID=31&SubSectionID=62&ArticleID=29033.

[20] Schnikey, Gary. "Anhydrous Ammonia, Corn, and Natural Gas Prices Over Time." *Farmdoc daily*, no. 6. (2016). 112. http://farmdocdaily.illinois.edu/2016/06/anhydrous-ammonia-corn-and-natural-gas-prices.html.

[21] Charles, Dan. "Why Lots Of Grass-Fed Beef Sold In U.S. Comes From Down Under." National Public Radio. October 3, 2013. Accessed November 15, 2018. https://www.npr.org/sections/thesalt/2013/10/04/228659915/why-most-grass-fed-beef-sold-in-u-s-comes-from-down-under.